FROM SPORTS *to* LIFE!

Scan QR code to unlock exclusive interview with NFL Super Bowl Champion Andrew Whitworth on why *From Sports to Life!* is the ultimate playbook for success.

FROM SPORTS
to LIFE!

Using Sports to Build Character,
Not Characters!

MARC MAYE

First edition
Printed in the United States
Library of Congress Control Number: 2025919288

Maye, Marc. From Sports to Life / Marc Maye. - 1. SEL027000 SELF-HELP / Personal Growth / Success; 2. SPO000000 SPORTS & RECREATION / General; 3. HEA046000 HEALTH & FITNESS / Children & Adolescents

ISBN 979-8-9930267-0-1 (paperback)
ISBN 979-8-9930267-1-8 (hardcover)
ISBN 979-8-9930267-2-5 (ebook)

Editing by Michael Tizzano
Cover/Interior Design by Danna Mathias Steele

DEDICATION

This book is dedicated to my beautiful mother, Areatha Maye. She is the reason for my existence and the reason why I do what I do. She helped me understand the true value of service, which ultimately led me to discover my life's purpose. May her soul rest in peace, and may her legacy continue forevermore.

Contents

Foreword #1

I first met Marc Maye in the summer of 2017 when I visited a youth camp he was running. At first, I decided to drop in, do the standard, demonstrate some skills, speak to the kids about the importance of working hard and leadership, and head home. But within minutes of stepping onto that court, I could see that something uniquely different was happening here. This wasn't just another sports camp. It was a place where the scoreboard wouldn't define success, but instead, teaching life skills was just as necessary as training for the game.

That day left a profound impression on me. The kids weren't just learning how to dribble or shoot; they were also learning how to lead, communicate, handle setbacks, and work as a team. They were learning all this from Marc, a man who sees sports as a vehicle to build character, not characters.

The following year, because of Marc's impact on me as well as the children, I didn't just stop by, but I joined Marc every single day of camp as a mentor and coach. I brought in some additional resources from the Lakers, but the real resource was Marc himself. His energy, his vision, and his unwavering belief in these kids were contagious. At the end of that camp, I told him what I knew in my gut: this camp was too important to wait another year to do again. We needed to build something that could live and breathe all year long.

That conversation became the seed for what is now the iPlayiLead Academy, a year-round after-school program that uses all sports to teach life skills and create wraparound support for kids and their families. I've been locked in with Marc on this vision ever since. I've seen him pour himself into this work, be present in the lives of these young people, and lead a movement that's as much about humanity as it is about athletics. I was there when he gave his TED Talk on this very subject, and I've watched his unwavering passion only grow deeper over the years.

From Sports to Life! is more than a book; it's a blueprint. It's a tool for every coach, mentor, and educator who believes their role is about more than wins and losses. In these pages, Marc shares real-life stories, the birth of the iPlayiLead Academy, powerful testimonies from coaches in the field, and most importantly, the voices of the youth themselves. He addresses the realities of trauma, environment, equity, and relationships as he empathizes with the young people due to his own personal upbringing. He offers a practical framework for teaching character, accountability, resilience, and purpose through sports.

Marc takes us beyond the stats and into the stories, revealing how competition can teach humility, how setbacks can build resilience, and how victories, big or small, can shape character for a lifetime. This is not theory; it's lived experience from a man who has stood on both the sidelines and the front lines of change.

I've spent most of my life around the game of basketball, and I can tell you: the lessons that stick with you long after the final buzzer are the ones about life. Marc understands this better than anyone I've met. His work reminds us that every coach is, in truth, a coach of life.

I've had the privilege of watching Marc work hands-on with the youth through sport, in the community, and provide academic support for the lives of young people who didn't always see their own potential.

Time after time, I've seen him use sports as a language of hope: speaking to kids who felt unheard, building bridges where there were once walls, and showing entire communities that teamwork, discipline, and perseverance can carry you further than talent alone ever will.

Whether you lead a team, a classroom, or a community, I encourage you to take in what Marc has written here. If you do, you'll walk away with more than just strategies; you'll walk away with a vision for shaping not only athletes, but also strong, grounded, resilient human beings. So I invite you to turn the page with an open mind and a willing heart. The lessons here may begin with sports, but their impact can reach every part of your life.

—Kurt Rambis
Los Angeles Lakers

Foreword #2

I have had the privilege of working in professional sports for 24 seasons and overseeing the Los Angeles Rams (previously the St. Louis Rams) community impact work since 2006. It's the greatest job in the world – utilizing our incredible platform to better our community. I often tell people that it's more than a job – it's my passion and my purpose. In my 24 seasons, I have been blessed to meet and work with countless amazing humans, but none more amazing than Marc Maye. There are those special times in life when you meet someone and are reminded of the goodness in the world. When I met Marc, I was blown away by his passion and heart. Throughout my career, I have encountered many individuals who made a strong first impression and presented themselves with passion and heart. Still, that fire often faded when the real work began.

As the General Manager of our Watts and Lincoln Rams, Marc is that unique individual who is energized by the work and consistently shows up when our young people need him. His consistency is a stabilizing force for many of our youth, who often lack consistency in their life. When the Los Angeles Rams adopted the former "Watts Bears" youth football program and renamed them the "Watts Rams" in 2018, the purpose of the program was to use the game of football to help bridge the divide between law enforcement and people of color by having police officers serve as the coaches of the youth football teams and allowing relationships to develop.

While that remains a primary goal today, with Marc's vision, we have been able to evolve beyond that singular focus to reach the kids and enrich their lives in ways that stretch far beyond the football field.

Marc and I often discuss the fact that football is the carrot that captures the attention of young people, and from there, we can wrap our arms around them, help develop their character, and inspire them to dream beyond their current realities. Under Marc's leadership, minds have been opened, life trajectories have been changed, and love and Human growth have become our north star..

I thank God every day for Marc. He's a unique leader who blends charisma with integrity, compassion, patience, empathy, and warmth. He inspires everyone around him to be a better human being. And with his growth mindset, he never allows himself to become complacent with past successes because he knows there is so much more work to be done...

—Molly Higgins
Executive Vice President, Community Impact
and Engagement, Los Angeles Rams
President, Los Angeles Rams Foundation

Summary of Key Components of this Book

- **Beyond Professional Athletes:** This book argues that with less than 2% of NCAA athletes turning professional, the focus in youth sports should shift from creating professional athletes to developing "professional"– well-rounded individuals prepared for life.

- **Transferable Skills:** This book highlights the importance of teaching "transferable skills," demonstrating how lessons learned in sports are directly applicable to life's challenges.

- **Understanding Youth Development:** A significant portion of the book is dedicated to understanding the adolescent brain and the physical, emotional, and social development stages of young people. This includes insights into brain plasticity, sensitivity to environmental cues, and the development of cognitive skills. The book also details four stages of brain development between ages 10 and 18: rapid growth and pruning (10-12 years), increased emotional sensitivity (12-14 years), identity and social development (13-16 years), and strengthening executive function (16-18 years).

- **Impact of Sports (Positive and Negative):** Sports can be a powerful vehicle for positive reinforcement, instilling discipline, structure, time management, and promoting overall well-being and social skills. However, it also acknowledges the potential for negative reinforcement through toxic coaching, excessive pressure, and prioritization of winning over character, which can lead to emotional trauma, burnout, and negative behaviors. The book stresses that sports are a tool whose impact depends on how they are used.

- **The Coach as Mentor and Teacher:** This book calls for a mindset shift among coaches to prioritize building people over just winning games. It differentiates between "major league" coaches (paid to win) and "minor league" coaches (paid to develop players), advocating for the latter approach in youth sports. "Champion coaches" are those who focus on effort, development, personal growth, and creating a safe and supportive culture.

- **iPlayiLead Academy Framework:** This book introduces the "iPlayiLead Academy" as a practical framework for integrating life skills into sports. This year-round program uses sports to teach resilience, responsibility, discipline, time management, leadership, conflict resolution, and goal setting through consistent programming, academic support, and community engagement. The Academy's structure includes dedicated time for mentorship, life skills workshops, skill development, and group reflection.

- **Trauma-Informed Approach and Equity:** This book highlights the importance of coaches' understanding of trauma-informed approaches and creating inclusive, culturally sensitive environments, especially for underserved youth who may have experienced trauma. It emphasizes the critical role of relationships between coaches and players, as well as among teammates, in fostering healthy connections and a sense of belonging.

- **Building Program Identity and Emotional Safety:** This emphasizes the importance of youth sports programs in establishing a strong identity founded on values such as respect, accountability, and compassion. Creating a culture of emotional safety, built on trust, belonging, and consistency, is presented as paramount. The "check-in" is highlighted as an underutilized tool for coaches to connect with youth and understand their struggles beyond the field.

HOW THIS BOOK SUPPORTS GROWTH AND DEVELOPMENT

- **Lack of Holistic Development:** Many coaches focus solely on winning, often at the expense of a child's overall development. This book offers a framework and philosophy for moving beyond this limited approach, demonstrating how to intentionally integrate life skills into sports.

- **Misunderstanding Youth Behavior:** This book addresses the pain point of coaches not understanding the developmental stages of youth, particularly the adolescent brain. By outlining cognitive, emotional, social, and physical development, it equips coaches to "meet young people where they are" and tailor their approach effectively.

- **Ineffective Coaching Strategies:** Coaches may struggle to convey abstract life skills tangibly. This book offers practical strategies, such as "Practice to Life drills," reflection exercises, and goal check-ins, to bridge the gap between sports and real-life application.

- **Dealing with Difficult Behaviors/Trauma:** This book directly addresses how coaches often misinterpret behaviors as "attitudes" or "disrespect" when they might be "calls for help" stemming from trauma. It advocates for trauma-informed approaches and prioritizes compassion over correction, offering a solution to better support youth facing adversity.

- **Building a Strong Team Culture:** Coaches may face challenges with team dynamics, such as cliques, competition-induced jealousy, and conflict. This book offers guidance on fostering healthy competition, breaking down cliques, and utilizing conflict as a teachable moment, emphasizing the creation of a supportive "family" environment founded on trust, belonging, and consistency.

- **Lack of Support System:** Youth programs often operate in isolation from one another. This book encourages collaboration with families, schools, and communities to establish a comprehensive support system for young people, emphasizing the need for a more integrated approach to youth development.

This book, "From Sports to Life! Using Sports to Build Character, Not Characters!" aims to guide coaches, mentors, and educators on how to leverage sports for youth development beyond athletic achievement. It emphasizes using sports as a "hook" to teach essential life skills, such as leadership, confidence, responsibility, resilience, and teamwork.

Why Sports Matter Beyond the Game of X's & O's

William James, the father of American psychology, reminds us that it is our job as instructors to tap into the natural interests of children to spark their ability to connect with the ideas we share.

Sports is just the hook—our way in—to teach leadership, confidence, respect, responsibility, attitude, resilience, teamwork, and more.

The purpose of this book is to inspire and motivate coaches, mentors, and educators on how to maximize the benefits of sports. Many young people participate in sports throughout their lives, yet they often still fall short once they become adults. The reason is that we are using sports on a minimal basis. Sports can propel young people into bright and successful futures, whether they reach the professional level or not. The goal should be to use sports to create professionals, not just professional athletes. Did you know that fewer than 2% of NCAA athletes go pro? There are nearly half a million NCAA athletes, and most will pursue careers that are not professional athletics. If that is indeed the case, then why don't we apply the same philosophy when coaching our kids during their developmental years? Why are we ok with just telling them they need a backup plan, but never really helping them develop the blueprint to that backup plan? Why does it even need to be a backup plan?

Why can't option 2 be as crucial as option 1? Why can't we help our youth understand that the same lessons they learn in sports are the same ones they will face in life? This book is not to put any coach, mentor, or educator down, but instead it's to lift you all and help us understand the power we have with sports and how the power of sports can be something all young people look at as a tool to help them navigate through their unique journeys of life. Too often, young people believe they fail at sports because they only have one end goal. When that "failure" hits, most young people don't know how to respond to it, as they often put all their eggs in one basket. The only failure that actually occurs is the failure to recognize that they already possess the tools for success. The failure lies in the application of what I call transferable skills, not failing at the game. Recognizing their transferable skills is not a failure of that young adolescent, but instead a failure of the coach or mentor.

Levels of Learning

When coaches and mentors educate themselves on the mental and physical development of young adolescent athletes, they recognize the significant role it plays in how they receive and apply information, leading to better outcomes. This is also evident in the educational levels of youth. For example, suppose a 6th-grade student is reading at a 3rd-grade level. In that case, it may be challenging for them to comprehend the material in the classroom and during practice if it's not differentiated to their level of understanding. Additionally, if a coach or mentor doesn't understand the difference between the three types of learners, they won't be able to effectively serve their youth. For example, the visual learner understands things from a visual perspective. As a coach, if you are only speaking at them, then they will never understand, and a disconnect will arise between the coach and the athlete regarding why things aren't being comprehended. This can ultimately result in losing games due to a lack of understanding of instructions and assignments. The same applies to auditory learners and kinesthetic learners. The auditory learner needs to hear the information, and for them, it will never matter how many times they see the instruction; their learning style requires them to hear it clearly. The Kinesthetic learner can listen to it a thousand times and still won't understand; they can see it another thousand times and still won't understand. Instead, they need to get to it as they are hands-on learners. Understanding this as a coach or mentor will set you and your team up for success on so many levels.

This book will also enable coaches and mentors to understand how sports can be used to teach life lessons. We call them transferable skills, and if used correctly, by breaking down the game in the most intense moments, you can help young people see those moments in different ways that relate to life outside of sports. I want young people to get back to having fun by playing the game, while also gaining impactful takeaways that help them view life's challenges and obstacles in a different light. If coaches aren't being intentional about those teachings, then we ultimately lose our kids, causing them to struggle and fail at our own expense. Coaches and mentors need to understand that saving lives should be the priority, and if that becomes our focus, then we will win games as a result. Not the other way around.

The Influence of Sports as a Universal Language and Tool for Mentorship

Coaches and mentors should understand that sports are a powerful metaphor for life and can be a valuable tool if used correctly. Sports break down walls and bring us all together. Not only does sports build exceptional character traits and values, but it also creates a safe space for people to unite. If that's the case for people, then why do we make that exception for our youth and focus on the opposite when it comes to them? We should find ways to lead with sports to create healthy dialogue with our youth that allows them to open up and become vulnerable in ways that we can reach them and deal with the underlying trauma they have and might not even know it.

We should allow sports to serve as the vehicle to teach and create life-changing moments. Many people say we know this, but do we truly practice it? I've seen coaches lead with this philosophy, but that's where it stops. We teach youth all the life lessons about sports, but we don't actually show them how they apply in life, because we expect them to understand from our instructions. This ties back to a point I made earlier about understanding our audience and the various types of learners. It also has a significant impact on the brain development of our youth, and if coaches don't understand or possess in-depth knowledge of this, then how can we claim to be truly reaching our youth?

A Call to Action for Coaches, Mentors, and Educators to Rise as Life-Shapers

My call to action is for all youth coaches and mentors to set aside their egos and hear me out. I speak from personal experience, having been the kid in this situation and grown into the coach I am now. It's all about growth, and growth occurs when we empathize and put ourselves in others' shoes. I had to put my grown self back in my shoes as a youth athlete and remind myself of the exact principles I am sharing today. I had to turn off my ego and turn on my intellect. Too many coaches are living vicariously through our kids because of their deferred dreams. Too many coaches blame society instead of themselves. Too many coaches are harming our youth because they fail to adjust and change with the times. Some coaches say, "Well, when I grew up, we did it this way, and I'm ok," But that's the thing, are we ok? I feel that too many of us coaches have unpacked trauma that we haven't dealt with yet, and we are putting it on the next generation and not breaking the cycle.

Too many coaches can't remove their own egos to admit that they aren't always right, and it shows up in how they deal with our youth. Perhaps if we acknowledge that we aren't right, we can see that the old ways actually don't work as we think they do. Now, don't get me wrong; I'm not saying we need to be soft and watered down. I'm suggesting that perhaps it's time to explore alternative approaches to dealing with our youth today. *Yes*, let's continue to teach discipline, resilience, perseverance, attitude, confidence, teamwork, and all the character traits that come with sports, but let's do it from a place that is whole, intentional, and adequately prescribed for the youth we are dealing with. It's not a one-size-fits-all prescription; it's a prescription tailored uniquely to each young person. Let's build winners on and off the field, but first let's hold ourselves accountable and build ourselves too.

PART I

Understanding the Adolescent Athlete

CHAPTER 1

The Adolescent Brain and Behavior

I recall a time when I worked as an educator, specifically during my tenure as Vice Principal and Dean of Discipline. The bell had barely rung when I got a call from the office staff: "Can you come grab one of your student-athletes from the office? He got into it with a teacher, again!"

I walked in and saw the young man, a 12-year-old sixth grader who played running back on our team, slouched in the chair with his hoodie up, arms crossed, eyes blank. He wasn't angry at all, but he wasn't present. Completely checked out.

The moment was familiar as he had refused to do his assignment, muttered something under his breath, then walked out of class when asked to stay behind. The teacher said he had an attitude. The office wrote him up. And now, here he was facing another suspension pending.

But before I took him back to class or made any further moves, I sat next to him and asked a simple question: "What's going on with you today?"

At first, silence. Then his eyes welled up. "Last night, we saw something bad happen in our neighborhood while we were outside playing. A fight happened right in front of us, and I think a man died because when we saw him on the ground, he wasn't moving, and later on, the police had yellow tape around." He hadn't eaten. He hadn't done his homework. He hadn't even changed clothes since yesterday.

And yet, here he was, expected to sit in a structured classroom, complete work, regulate his emotions, and follow directions while his world outside those school walls was all over the place.

That moment reminded me of something we can't afford to ignore: adolescent behavior is rarely just about behavior. Behind every eye roll, outburst, or shutdown is a brain still trying to make sense of life, a nervous system learning how to respond to stress, and often a young person silently asking for help in the only way they know how.

Whether in the classroom or on the field, we must remember that our kids' brains are still under construction. Their emotional outbursts, their impulsive choices, and their inconsistencies are not just "bad attitudes" or "disrespect." They're signals and warnings, cries for support.

This is why it's not enough for us to be just coaches, educators, or mentors. We must become students of the adolescent brain. Because if we don't understand how they're wired, we risk mislabeling growth as misbehavior, and we lose moments to truly help them.

This upcoming chapter isn't about excuses. It's about understanding. It's about shifting how we view our youth so we can better support them, not just as athletes, but as developing humans. Because when we understand their brain, we begin to understand their behavior. And when we know their behavior, we create space for growth, healing, and transformation, whether it be on or off the field.

Understanding the way the adolescent brain works can be key to understanding certain behaviors in our youth. The following two chapters will outline the key concepts of how the brain develops amongst youth and how youth grow from a physical, cognitive, and emotional breakdown, which will also help us understand the social development of our youth. These are essential things to know, as they will better our understanding as coaches and allow us to meet our young people where they are at that exact moment. When you understand a person's development standpoint, you can prescribe the right tools for that individual's success. This is so important for us as coaches because we must constantly remind ourselves that we are coaching our young people in sports, but ultimately, we are coaching them for life.

The brain experiences a period of remarkable **plasticity.** This occurs because, during adolescence, the brain is highly flexible, adaptable, and capable of rapid change. Plasticity refers to the brain's ability to rewire itself, form new connections, and strengthen or weaken existing ones based on experience. During adolescence (roughly ages 10–25), the brain goes through a significant transformation. It's not just growing, but it's actually remodeling itself. This is a time when young people are particularly adept at acquiring new skills, adapting to challenges, and forming their identity. This is important for us to understand because positive influences, such as mentorship, education, and healthy relationships, can have a lasting impact on individuals. At the same time, negative experiences (like trauma, substance use, or chronic stress) can also strongly affect adolescent brain development. So, teenage brain plasticity is both an opportunity and a responsibility. It's a window where young people are extremely moldable, but the question for us as coaches and mentors is, will it be for better or worse?

The brain is also susceptib**le to environmental cues.** Meaning teens and young people are especially influenced by the world around them, such as the people, places, situations, and messages they experience daily. Environmental cues are signals from the environment, such as peer pressure, social media, family dynamics, community norms, or even music and pop culture. The adolescent brain is still developing, especially in areas responsible for decision-making, self-control, and emotional regulation. Because of this, teens are more reactive to what's happening around them and more likely to adapt their behavior based on those signals.

This matters because if the adolescent brain is surrounded by positive influences such as supportive mentors, safe environments, and positive peer groups, youth are more likely to make healthy choices and develop strong character. Suppose they are surrounded by negative cues like violence, pressure to use drugs, and unhealthy role models. In that case, they are more likely to exhibit that behavior or be emotionally and mentally affected. So, this sensitivity is a powerful reminder that what we expose young people to matters deeply as they're paying attention, absorbing it, and often letting it shape who they're becoming.

The brain experiences tremendous **growth in cognitive skills.** This is mainly because during the teenage years, young people go through a significant leap in their ability to think, reason, and understand the world. Cognitive skills refer to the brain's mental abilities, such as problem-solving, critical thinking, decision-making, understanding consequences, planning, and self-reflection. During adolescence, the prefrontal cortex, a part of the brain responsible for higher-level thinking skills, rapidly develops and becomes more efficient. This matters because it allows us, as coaches and mentors, to understand that teens begin to think more deeply and abstractly, and start asking big questions about life, identity, justice, and purpose. They can weigh the pros and cons, consider different perspectives, and start making independent choices. This growth helps prepare them for adulthood, but because the brain is still developing, they may also struggle with impulse control or consistency in decision-making. In short, adolescence is a time of mental growth and exploration, during which young people build the tools they'll need to think for themselves and navigate the real world.

Brain development between ages 10–18 (The four stages of growth)

Brain development between the ages of 10 and 18 is a critical and transformative period in a person's life. The brain doesn't just grow in size as it reorganizes, strengthens connections, and becomes more efficient, especially in areas related to thinking, emotions, and behavior. I want to share with you a simple breakdown of what happens during these stages, which you can use as a guide.

STAGE 1: RAPID GROWTH AND PRUNING (10–12 YEARS)

At this stage, brain cells increase as the brain builds new connections based on experiences. Then, it begins a process called "synaptic pruning," which is cutting away weak or unused connections to make the brain more efficient. A way to think about it is like clearing out clutter, allowing the brain to run smoothly.

What coaches and mentors can look for during this stage:

During the rapid growth and pruning stage of brain development (ages 10–12), coaches and mentors may notice kids displaying mood swings, sensitivity to criticism, or inconsistent focus. One moment, they may be locked in and thriving; the next, they're withdrawn or easily frustrated, especially after making mistakes. Coaches might also see a strong desire for peer approval, hesitation to take risks, or increased self-consciousness. These are all signs that the brain is reorganizing, and adults should respond with patience, structure, and encouragement by striking a balance between discipline and empathy to help kids feel safe as they grow.

STAGE 2: INCREASED EMOTIONAL SENSITIVITY (12-14 YEARS)

The amygdala, which plays a crucial role in controlling emotions, is highly active. During this stage, teens feel emotions more intensely. However, the prefrontal cortex, which we discussed earlier and is responsible for logic, planning, and impulse control, remains underdeveloped at this stage. This is why teens may react emotionally or take more risks, as they feel deeply but haven't yet fully developed self-regulation.

What coaches and mentors can look for during this stage:

During the ages of 12–14, when emotional sensitivity in brain development increases, coaches may notice kids taking things more personally, such as overreacting to criticism, shutting down after a mistake, or appearing embarrassed in front of their peers. They may become more concerned with how others perceive them and show signs of pulling away or lashing out when they feel misunderstood. A coach or mentor should look for changes in attitude, sudden quietness, or overly defensive responses, and respond with consistent support, clear communication, and a calm tone to help them feel respected and emotionally safe while still holding them accountable.

STAGE 3: IDENTITY AND SOCIAL DEVELOPMENT (13-16 YEARS)

As mentioned earlier in the chapter, the brain begins to tune in more to social cues, such as fitting in, seeking peer approval, and developing one's own identity, which become primary focuses. Their abstract thinking improves, and teens begin to grasp concepts such as justice, morality, and the long-term consequences of their actions. Kids start asking questions like "Who am I?" and "What do I believe?"

What coaches and mentors can look for during this stage:

Between the ages of 13 and 16, when children are in the identity and social development stage of brain growth, coaches may notice players experimenting with different personas, such as trying to "fit in" with their peers, asserting independence, or challenging authority more frequently. They might question rules, compare themselves to others, or show a deep need to be seen and valued beyond just their performance. Coaches should look out for shifts in confidence, sudden changes in behavior or friend groups, or kids who become more vocal about their beliefs and values. This is a critical time to reinforce a positive identity, provide mentorship, and create space for healthy self-expression while maintaining a strong team structure.

STAGE 4: STRENGTHENING EXECUTIVE FUNCTION (17–18 YEARS)

In the final stage of adolescence, the prefrontal cortex continues to mature, and skills such as goal setting, time management, impulse control, and decision-making further develop and improve. However, they're not fully developed until the mid-20s.

What coaches and mentors can look for during this stage:

At ages 17–18, when the brain is developing executive function, coaches may notice players exhibiting more self-awareness, improved decision-making, and greater responsibility both on and off the field. They may begin to think ahead, manage emotions more effectively, and take ownership of their actions. However, lapses still occur, such as procrastination, inconsistent focus, or overconfidence. Coaches and mentors should look for signs of leadership potential, more thoughtful communication, and a growing ability to reflect on mistakes. This is a prime time to challenge them with real responsibility while guiding them toward consistent maturity and accountability.

In conclusion, the adolescent brain is akin to a construction zone, which means it's under development, rapidly changing, and highly sensitive to its environment. Experiences during this time, whether they are positive or negative, can shape long-term behavior and mental health. Youth need guidance, structure, and support, not because they're incapable, but because their brains are still learning how to lead. Sports can have a profound influence on the development of young adolescents in ways that are both physical and psychological, as well as emotionally and socially. Depending on the specific environment, coaching style, and peer dynamics, sports can either positively support growth or reinforce negative patterns of behavior.

Positive Reinforcement Through Sports

Sports serve as a powerful vehicle for positive reinforcement in the lives of young people, instilling discipline and structure through regular practices, clear rules, and consistent routines. This environment teaches teens time management, self-control, and the importance of commitment, while helping them work toward goals and manage responsibilities. Beyond the physical benefits, sports promote overall well-being by improving fitness, reducing stress, and enhancing brain function. The release of endorphins supports emotional regulation and helps combat anxiety and depression.

Participation also strengthens social skills and teamwork by fostering communication, cooperation, empathy, and leadership within group dynamics. As teens experience growth and success in sports, their confidence and sense of identity are reinforced, shaping self-perceptions such as "I'm a hard worker" or "I'm a team player." Additionally, the presence of coaches and mentors provides consistent, positive adult influence by modeling respect, resilience, and accountability, which ultimately acts as a protective factor against negative influences and supports healthy development.

Negative Reinforcement Through Sports

While sports can be a source of growth, they can also reinforce negative behaviors and mindsets when not adequately managed. Toxic coaching or poor role models, such as those who rely on fear, shame, or favoritism, can damage a teen's self-esteem and even create lasting emotional trauma. When winning is prioritized over character, young athletes may internalize harmful messages, such as the belief that success matters more than integrity. Excessive pressure and unrealistic expectations, including overtraining, can lead to stress, anxiety, burnout, and a loss of passion for the game.

In these environments, teens may begin to tie their self-worth solely to performance, causing identity struggles when they fall short. Additionally, when aggression, cheating, or poor sportsmanship are tolerated or rewarded, these behaviors can become normalized, teaching that domination is more valuable than collaboration. Finally, exclusion or inequality, whether through favoritism or a lack of inclusion, can leave youth feeling isolated, judged, and undervalued, which reinforces division, bias, and low self-esteem.

Sports are a tool. Whether they build or break depends on how that tool is used and guided. When structured well, sports can be one of the most transformative experiences in an adolescent's life, which becomes essential for developing character, resilience, and leadership. If you're working with youth in sports, the culture you build is just as crucial as the drills you run. My final point of this chapter is to note that the brain has a natural negativity bias, and positive language can resist it and rewrite it. Let's show up for our youth the right way and give the game back to them by using sports for more than just creating professional athletes, but instead for creating skilled individuals.

MAYE'S 5 KEY CHAPTER TAKEAWAYS: CHAPTER 1

1. Adolescence is a critical stage of brain development (ages 10–25): The brain is highly plastic during this period, meaning that experiences—positive or negative—can significantly shape identity, behavior, and long-term growth.

2. Environmental influences matter deeply: Teens are susceptible to cues from peers, family, mentors, media, and community. Supportive environments promote healthy choices, while negative influences increase risk for harmful behaviors.

3. Cognitive and emotional growth is uneven: While the prefrontal cortex (responsible for reasoning, planning, and self-control) is still developing, the emotional centers of the brain are highly active, which can lead to impulsive or reactive behavior.

4. Brain development progresses in stages (10–18): Each stage (growth and pruning, emotional sensitivity, identity/social development, and executive function strengthening) presents unique challenges and opportunities that coaches and mentors should recognize and respond to with patience, structure, and guidance.

5. Sports can build or break youth development: When led with positive reinforcement, sports foster discipline, resilience, confidence, and character. But poor coaching or toxic cultures can cause lasting harm, reinforcing stress, low self-worth, or unhealthy behaviors.

I remember a kid named Mick, who was quiet, lanky, and always the last one to walk into practice. He was in sixth grade when he joined our team, barely spoke above a whisper, and looked like he didn't believe he belonged. Physically, he was behind the other kids as he was thin, awkward in his movements, and struggling with basic drills. Emotionally, he carried himself like someone who had already given up on being chosen. Socially, he stayed to himself, never laughed, never connected. For weeks, he didn't stand out. But we kept showing up for him.

We gave him small wins. We celebrated effort. We assigned him to a mentor on the team who made it his mission to bring Mick out of his shell. Slowly, Mick began to change and not just as a player, but as a person. His coordination improved. His posture shifted. He started talking more. Then one day after practice, he came up to me and said, "Coach, I made two friends today… real friends."

That moment had nothing to do with basketball and everything to do with development. What we often forget is that sports are about far more than just talent or competition. It's a training ground for the whole child, which includes the body, mind, and relationships. It's one of the few environments where physical growth, emotional resilience, and social confidence can all be nurtured simultaneously, but only if we know what we're looking for.

This chapter explores the underlying factors that influence the growth of children, including why some may be physically behind, others may be emotionally volatile, and how peer relationships can either support or hinder a young athlete's development. When we educate ourselves on these developmental layers, we stop judging kids for where they aren't and start helping them for where they are.

Because a child's development doesn't happen in a straight line, it's messy and unique. And when we meet them with understanding and intentionality, we don't just develop better athletes, we ultimately develop better human beings.

CHAPTER 2

Physical, Emotional & Social Development

Sports offer a unique and powerful platform for the physical, emotional, and social development of young people. From emotional regulation and self-awareness to the impact of peer dynamics in team settings, young athletes are continually learning how to navigate life's complexities through play and competition. The locker room often serves as a microcosm of society, where youth build relationships, learn to communicate, and experience the ups and downs of human interaction.

Coaches play a critical role in this process by not only guiding physical development but also modeling empathy, resilience, and effective communication. However, to coach in truly impactful ways, we must first understand the developmental stages that young people go through. Without a clear grasp of how youth grow cognitively, emotionally, and socially, it becomes nearly impossible to meet them where they are and support their progress effectively. This understanding is essential for any coach committed to nurturing the whole athlete, encompassing not only their performance but also their personal growth.

Here's a breakdown of **child development stages by age** with a focus on **cognitive, emotional, and social understanding**. To me, this is one of the keys to success when it comes to serving and reaching developing youth.

1. Infancy (1–2 years)

UNDERSTANDING:

- **Cognitive:** Learning through senses and movement (sensorimotor stage).
- **Emotional:** Begins to form attachment to caregivers; expresses basic emotions (joy, fear, anger).
- **Social:** Recognizes familiar faces; develops trust when needs are consistently met.

KEY NEEDS:

- Consistency
- Physical affection
- Safe exploration

2. Early Childhood (2–5 years)

UNDERSTANDING:

- **Cognitive:** Rapid language development; begins to understand symbols and pretend play (preoperational stage).
- **Emotional:** Learns to name emotions; struggles with emotional regulation.
- **Social:** Plays alongside others (parallel play → cooperative play); starts to understand rules but is still very self-centered.

KEY NEEDS:

- Clear boundaries
- Encouragement of imagination
- Support in naming and managing emotions

3. Early School Age (5–8 years)

UNDERSTANDING:

- **Cognitive:** Can think more logically about concrete events (concrete operational starts around 7).
- **Emotional:** Begins to grasp empathy; needs help understanding and expressing complex feelings.
- **Social:** Seeks approval from adults; peer relationships become more meaningful.

KEY NEEDS:

- Recognition and encouragement
- Structure and routine
- Opportunities for peer interaction and team activities

4. Middle Childhood (9–11 years)

UNDERSTANDING:

- **Cognitive:** Better understanding of cause and effect, time, and consequences.
- **Emotional:** Begins to internalize values; can compare self to others and may develop self-doubt.
- **Social:** Stronger peer influence; friendships based on trust and loyalty.

KEY NEEDS:

- Opportunities for responsibility
- Positive role models
- Safe space for self-expression and building confidence

5. Early Adolescence (12–14 years)

UNDERSTANDING:

- **Cognitive:** Beginning of abstract thinking (formal operational stage); questions rules and authority.
- **Emotional:** Mood swings; forming identity; seeks independence while needing guidance.
- **Social:** Peer approval is critical; desire to "fit in" can outweigh logic.

KEY NEEDS:

- Respect and autonomy
- Open dialogue and guidance
- Mentorship that balances accountability with empathy

6. Middle Adolescence (15–17 years)

UNDERSTANDING:

- **Cognitive:** Improved reasoning and future-thinking; can consider multiple perspectives.
- **Emotional:** Identity solidifies; values and beliefs begin to take shape.
- **Social:** Intimate friendships and relationships emerge; may challenge norms or test limits.

KEY NEEDS:

- Deep conversations about life choices
- Career and purpose-focused guidance
- Real-world experiences and mentorship

Age Range	Understanding	Key Needs
Infancy (0–2 years)	**Cognitive:** Learning through senses and movement. **Emotional:** Forms attachments; expresses basic emotions. **Social:** Recognizes faces; develops trust.	Consistency, physical affection, safe exploration.
Early Childhood (2–5 years)	Cognitive: Rapid language development; symbolic play. Emotional: Learns to name emotions; struggles with regulation. Social: Parallel to cooperative play; begins to understand rules.	Clear boundaries, encouragement of imagination, support in managing emotions.
Early School Age (5–8 years)	Cognitive: More logical thinking about concrete events. Emotional: Grasps empathy; needs help with complex feelings. Social: Seeks adult approval; peer relationships grow.	Recognition and encouragement, structure and routine, opportunities for peer/team activities.
Middle Childhood (9–11 years)	Cognitive: Better understanding of cause, effect, time, consequences. Emotional: Internalizes values; may develop self-doubt. Social: Stronger peer influence; friendships based on trust.	Opportunities for responsibility, positive role models, safe space for self-expression and confidence.
Early Adolescence (12–14 years)	Cognitive: Abstract thinking begins; questions rules/authority. Emotional: Mood swings; identity formation; seeks independence. Social: Peer approval is critical; desire to "fit in."	Respect and autonomy, open dialogue and guidance, mentorship balancing accountability with empathy.
Middle Adolescence (15–17 years)	Cognitive: Improved reasoning and future-thinking; considers multiple perspectives. Emotional: Identity solidifies; values and beliefs form. Social: Intimate friendships; may challenge norms.	Deep conversations about life choices, career/purpose-focused guidance, real-world experiences and mentorship.

Physical Development among Adolescents

Physical growth in young people varies significantly by age and stage of development, and recognizing these changes is essential for effective coaching. Between the ages of 7 and 11, youth are gradually building strength and stamina, but still require ample recovery time and proper cool-downs to support their growing bodies. During this stage, the focus should remain on mastering basic movement patterns and fundamental skills rather than pushing intense physical demands.

As youth enter adolescence, typically around age 12 and older, many begin to experience growth spurts and increased muscle development. At this stage, they are better equipped to handle more physical challenges, allowing coaches to introduce more complex skills and higher levels of training intensity. Understanding these physical milestones ensures that young athletes are supported in a way that promotes long-term health, development, and a positive relationship with sports.

In conclusion, understanding the stages of physical, cognitive, and social development is essential for anyone working with young athletes. As youth grow, they progress through distinct phases of thinking and relating to others. In the early stages, they often believe that everyone sees the world as they do, and they work side by side without genuine collaboration. In the middle stages, they begin to recognize that others think differently and start developing the skills to communicate, strategize, and engage with teammates and opponents.

By the latter stages, they can empathize, put themselves in others' shoes, and apply values like fairness and respect while living out the golden rule. As coaches and mentors, recognizing where each young person is in this progression allows us to teach, guide, and support them in ways that align with their developmental needs. When we do this well, sports become more than just a game; they become a space for real growth, connection, and lifelong learning.

MAYE'S 5 KEY CHAPTER
TAKEAWAYS: CHAPTER 2

1. **Sports are more than physical activity:** They provide a platform for emotional regulation, self-awareness, communication, and social growth, making the locker room a training ground for life skills.

2. **Coaches influence whole-person development:** Effective coaching goes beyond athletic performance, requiring an understanding of cognitive, emotional, and social stages to nurture character, resilience, and empathy.

3. **Child and adolescent development occurs in stages.** From infancy through middle adolescence, each phase presents unique cognitive, emotional, and social needs that shape how young people learn, relate to others, and develop their identity.

4. **Physical development must align with training:** Younger athletes (7–11) need to focus on fundamentals and recovery, while adolescents (12+) can handle more complex skills as their bodies mature, highlighting the importance of age-appropriate coaching.

5. **Meeting youth where they are builds lasting impact:** When coaches and mentors tailor guidance to developmental stages, sports evolve into powerful environments for growth, connection, and lifelong learning.

His name was Ian. Twelve years old. Fast, explosive, and full of raw talent. On the field, he looked like a future star. But off the field, there was a heaviness in his eyes that told a different story. He rarely smiled. He kept his distance from teammates. And anytime a coach raised their voice, even slightly, you could see him flinch, not physically, but emotionally.

One day during practice, I suddenly blew up during a basic drill. Another player bumped into him, and he snapped, beginning to yell, push, and was ready to fight. Some of the coaches were quick to call it disrespect, label him "a problem," and threaten to suspend him.

I saw something else.

After practice, I pulled Ian aside and asked him, "What's really going on?" He broke down. Through tears, he shared that the night before, his older brother had been arrested right in front of him. He hadn't slept. The yelling on the field reminded him of how things sound when police show up at his door. Football wasn't the issue, but life was.

That moment changed everything for me. It reminded me that kids don't leave their trauma at the gate when they come to practice. The environment they live in, the fear, the instability, the inequality follow them into every drill, every locker room, every huddle. And unless we as coaches, mentors, and program leaders understand that reality, we'll miss the opportunity to be part of their healing.

Sports have the power to transform lives, but only if we acknowledge the whole picture: the trauma some kids carry, the environments they survive, the relationships that shape their self-worth, and the systems that don't always treat every child equally.

This chapter is about waking up to that truth. It's about shifting from judgment to understanding, from reaction to relationship. Because if we're truly here for the kids, we have to see all of them, not just the athlete, but the human being underneath. Only then can we create sports programs that are not only competitive but also compassionate, equitable, and life-changing.

CHAPTER 3

Trauma, Environment, Relationships, and Equity in Sports

Youth sports can be a powerful tool for healing and stability, especially for young people who have experienced trauma or adverse childhood experiences (ACEs). Many underserved and high-risk youth face challenges far beyond the playing field, such as poverty, community violence, unstable home environments, or systemic neglect. These experiences often affect how they regulate emotions, build trust, and respond to authority. For these youth, sports can become a haven, offering consistency, structure, and a sense of belonging that may be lacking in other areas of their lives.

A caring coach, a supportive team, and a predictable practice routine can serve as a grounding force, helping youth rebuild their sense of safety and self-worth. However, this requires coaches and mentors to understand trauma-informed approaches and meet young athletes with empathy rather than punishment, patience rather than pressure. It's not just about improving performance; it's about recognizing the emotional and psychological burdens some youth carry and using sports as a vehicle for stability, healing, and empowerment.

Equity, cultural sensitivity, and inclusive practices must also be central to how we engage youth in athletic spaces. Too often, sports environments unintentionally reflect the same inequalities found in society, where certain voices are silenced, certain styles are misunderstood, and certain athletes are overlooked. Coaches must be intentional about creating inclusive team cultures that value every young person's background, identity, and lived experience. This includes being aware of racial, gender, and socioeconomic disparities that might influence access to resources, playing time, or mentorship.

Furthermore, relationships are a critical area for growth in young athletes, especially in environments where positive adult figures are limited. The bonds formed between coaches and players, as well as among teammates themselves, can model healthy, respectful, and empathetic human connections. When done right, sports become more than just games, and as a result, they become spaces where young people feel seen, heard, and valued, laying the foundation not only for athletic success but also for lifelong social and emotional development.

In youth sports, youth are just beginning to understand what it means to have close friends. They are also just beginning to understand what it means to belong to a group outside of their family. If teams are like families, then all children should be treated by their teammates not only with respect but with genuine caring.

My goal is to emphasize not only relationships within the team, but relationships to family, classmates, and peers, which are built on a sense of fairness and sportsmanship. Our youth must build relationships of fairness, trust, caring, and respect. When that is done, we should then teach our youth what it looks like when they are on a team and how our team must be built with a sense of "Family". We can then teach them how to adopt the same approach with opponents and officials, and instruct them on maintaining healthy competition within the game itself. When we do that, our outcomes become a result of unity and cohesion with our teammates, as well as great sportsmanship towards opponents and officials.

MAYE'S 5 KEY CHAPTER TAKEAWAYS: CHAPTER 3

1. **Sports as healing spaces:** For youth facing trauma or adverse experiences, sports can provide stability, structure, and a sense of belonging, helping them rebuild trust, safety, and self-worth.

2. **Trauma-informed coaching matters:** Coaches should respond with empathy, patience, and understanding rather than punishment or pressure, recognizing the emotional burdens youth may carry.

3. **Equity and inclusion are essential:** Coaches must intentionally create team cultures that value diversity, address disparities, and ensure every athlete feels seen, heard, and respected.

4. **Relationships shape growth:** Positive bonds with coaches, teammates, and peers foster healthy connections, modeling respect, empathy, and trust that extend beyond the sports arena.

5. **Sportsmanship as a family culture:** Teaching fairness, caring, and respect within teams fosters unity, while extending that respect to opponents and officials lays a foundation for lifelong character and integrity.

PART II

The Framework – Using Sports to Build Life Skills

Life Skills & Sports- The Birth and Power of the iPlayiLead Academy & Project Blue

It was a regular weeknight practice. The kids were bouncing with energy, their shoes squeaking on the court, and the usual sounds of laughter and competitiveness filled the gym. But this session had a purpose beyond jump shots and agility drills. That night's life skill focus was Respect.

We built the concept into everything we did, from fun partner drills that emphasized communication and encouragement, team challenges where kids had to work together and lift each other, and a short group discussion where we broke down what respect really means: for yourself, for others, for your space, and even for the game.

We ended the session with a challenge, which is essentially homework. Nothing fancy, but just a simple request: Go out and try to live out this skill. At home. At school. In your everyday life. We told the kids that respect isn't just something you turn on at practice, but it's something that should show up wherever you go.

A few days later, my phone rang. It was one of our parents. I could tell by the tone in her voice that this wasn't just a routine call.

She asked, "Coach... was your lesson last week about respect or something close to it?"

I confirmed it, and she just started laughing in amazement. "My son has been on a whole different level. He's been saying 'yes ma'am,' asking how he can help around the house, being more patient with his little sister... even his teachers have noticed. I'm blown away. I've been trying to teach him this at home, but he actually got it through y'all."

*That moment said everything about why we built **iPlayiLead Academy**. She had enrolled her son, thinking this was just another sports program and something to keep him active and off the couch. What she discovered was something more profound: a space that used the structure of sports to build values, habits, and character.*

But it wasn't just her son who grew. She told us the program was also helping her and providing new ways to connect with her child, reinforcing the lessons she was trying to teach at home, and creating a bridge between the parent she aspired to be and the young woman she was becoming. Moments like that don't show up on a scoreboard, but they're the wins that matter most.

*This next chapter breaks down how the **iPlayiLead Academy** came to be, and how we've committed ourselves to using sports as a tool, not just for performance, but for purpose. Every coach, every session, every drill is designed with intention. Because when kids walk into our program, they may come for the sport, but they leave with life tools and a belief in the best version of themselves, on and off the court.*

The ***iPlayiLead Academy*** was born out of a vision I had to create more than just another youth sports camp. I wanted to build a transformative experience where sports served as the gateway to learning real-life skills. I cofounded the initiative in 2017, initially as a summer camp under the name *Playit4wrd*, using basketball as the bait to draw in youth, but the true purpose was much deeper. Each day of the camp was grounded in a life skill or pillar that was woven into every element of the experience, from the drills to the guest speakers to the small group reflections. The goal was to help kids understand that what they were doing on the court was directly connected to their experiences at home, in school, and in the world.

The structure was intentional: every lesson, every challenge, every game was an opportunity for a teaching moment. And the real magic happened when we slowed the game down. In this environment, we were able to pause, break down what just happened, and connect it to a life principle, which is something that never happens in real-time games. Even more powerful, the kids began to recognize those moments themselves, calling them out mid-play with excitement. We even incentivized this awareness, making learning and growth not only meaningful but also fun.

That first summer in 2017 was unforgettable, but what elevated it to a whole new level was an unexpected guest: NBA Laker legend Kurt Rambis. Introduced to me through a mutual friend, Kurt graciously joined us on the last day of camp, speaking to the youth about leadership and then demonstrating it through on-court drills. While the kids didn't immediately grasp the magnitude of who he was, their parents were in awe, and later, so were they, once they Googled him. At the end of that session, Kurt pulled me aside and asked if I was planning to rerun the camp the following summer. I said yes. He told me to expect a call.

True to his word, a month before camp in 2018, I got a call from an unknown number: "Hello Marc, it's me, Kurt!" He was back in L.A., working with the Lakers, and offered to bring the Laker Girls and basketballs for every camper. That summer, he didn't just show up; he worked alongside us daily, fully engaged with the campers. On the last day of the camp, Kurt challenged me with a question that changed everything: "Are you really going to wait another year to do something this powerful again?" That one conversation led to the birth of *iPlayiLead Academy,* a year-round, holistic program that expanded on the foundation of our summer camp. We built a model rooted in consistent programming, academic support, data tracking, community service, mentorship, and real-life skill-building, all through the lens of sports. No longer just a camp, the *iPlayiLead Academy* became a movement.

Today, we serve the youth of Compton, Watts, and South Los Angeles with weekly programs, weekend activations, field trips, family engagement, and relationship-building with local stakeholders and law enforcement. Our mission is simple but powerful: to use sports to build character, not characters, and to teach transferable life skills in a way that's fun, relatable, and life-changing. Kurt Rambis remains one of our founding visionaries and most dedicated supporters, and what started as a summer experiment is now a year-round blueprint for youth development, empowerment, and transformation.

At the heart of the *iPlayiLead Academy* lies a commitment to developing more than just athletes, as we are focused on building whole individuals. Every week, our programming is centered around key life principles that are essential not only for success in sports but for thriving in life: resilience, responsibility, discipline, time management, leadership, conflict resolution, and goal setting. These aren't just buzzwords we hang on the walls or sprinkle into conversations, but they are values we intentionally teach, model, and reinforce through every drill, huddle, and discussion. We believe that when these values are taught consistently and in context, they become habits. And when youth form strong habits early, they begin to navigate life with confidence, direction, and purpose.

In sports, resilience shows up every time a player misses a shot, loses a game, or faces a setback. In our Academy, we use these moments to remind youth that failure isn't final, but it's a step in the process of growth. We coach them to bounce back, not shut down. Responsibility is taught by having each player show up prepared, take care of their gear, be accountable to their teammates, and own their actions, whether good or bad. Discipline is found in repetition, in listening to coaching, and in the willingness to do the right thing even when no one is watching. Time management shows up when a young person learns to balance practice, school, homework, and rest, and begins to understand that success in any area requires the ability to prioritize. These are foundational life skills, and through sports, they become tangible and real.

We also make it a priority to instill leadership, conflict resolution, and goal setting, which are three pillars that are essential for youth to grow into empowered, self-aware individuals. Leadership is taught both vocally and by example. Players learn that leading doesn't always mean being the loudest, but it means being responsible, lifting others, and modeling the correct behavior even when it's hard. Conflict resolution is integrated into team dynamics where disagreements, frustrations, and misunderstandings are inevitable. We teach children how to listen, communicate respectfully, and find solutions that benefit the group. And finally, goal setting is something we revisit on a weekly basis.

Whether it's making five free throws in a row or improving a report card grade, we help each youth identify a personal target, map a plan, and take consistent steps toward it. These principles aren't taught in isolation, but they are woven into our practices, scrimmages, and classroom discussions. When a player sets a goal, gets frustrated, falls short, recalibrates, and tries again, they are living all these principles in motion. That's where the growth happens.

By embedding these lessons consistently into our weekly rhythm, we aren't just training athletes; instead, we're building a generation of young people who know how to lead, overcome, and take control of their futures. These life skills aren't extras; they're essentials. Through the structure of *iPlayiLead Academy,* we ensure that every child has a consistent, supportive environment where these values are not only taught but also lived. This is what makes our program transformative and necessary. It's not just about the game; it's about preparing youth for the bigger game called life.

The structure of the *iPlayiLead Academy* is intentionally designed to nurture the whole child, encompassing mind, body, and spirit, through a consistent and holistic approach. Each session begins with a dedicated hour focused on mentorship and life skills workshops, creating a safe space where youth can openly or anonymously share challenges they've faced during the week. This part of the program is sacred as it's where emotional regulation, vulnerability, and support come to life. Whether it's a conflict at home, stress from school, or personal struggles, we give young people the opportunity to process their feelings, receive guidance, and learn tools to manage their emotions in healthy ways. This therapeutic approach allows students to arrive more focused and connected. The next hour and a half are dedicated to skill development across various sports, including basketball, football, soccer, volleyball, golf, and self-defense, while ensuring we cater to diverse interests and talents.

The Academy also offers weekly Yoga and Art classes during this session for athletes who might need a mental break for the day or for students who don't always want to participate in a sport but appreciate the social offering of the program. This portion challenges them physically & mentally while reinforcing the life principles taught earlier. We conclude each session with a 30-minute wrap-up, during which all students come together to reflect on what they've learned, connect their experiences to real-life situations, and engage in a group resiliency conversation. This is also our time to celebrate wins such as academic progress, personal breakthroughs, or on-the-field highlights to boost confidence and reinforce positive behaviors. Youth leave with actionable steps to apply throughout the week and are encouraged to come back and share how those steps impacted them.

This structure not only helps develop well-rounded young people but also strengthens family connections. Parents frequently call us to share how the topics we discuss have opened doors to meaningful conversations at home, helping them parent more effectively. It's a win-win model as it's transforming not just youth, but entire families and communities.

The *iPlay iLead Academy* now thrives under the umbrella of **Project Blue**, an organization dedicated to bringing together people, resources, and partners to create genuine opportunities for underserved youth. This partnership has enabled *iPlay iLead* to expand its reach and impact, demonstrating that when collaboration is intentional, youth development programs can do far more than just provide a place to play; they can open doors, shape futures, and rewrite the narrative of what success looks like.

What makes **Project Blue** unique is its belief that we are stronger together. Too often, organizations work in silos, each doing good work but creating only a limited impact. **Project Blue** disrupts that model by uniting programs under a shared vision and guiding principles: Convening, Elevating, Amplifying, and Communicating (CEAC). These principles are not just words on paper; they form the foundation for transforming traditional, short-term activities into comprehensive, year-round programs.

Under this framework, the *iPlay iLead Academy, the Watts Rams, Lincoln Rams, Marching Beauties, and the Youth Leadership Council* have grown into holistic initiatives that support the "whole child." Sports, play, and recreation remain at the center, but they are used as a powerful hook to engage young people and draw them in. Once involved, youth gain far more than athletic skills. They develop life skills, leadership, confidence, discipline, and the mindset needed to succeed in any field of life. The result is a generation of young people prepared not just to compete on the field, but to thrive in the classroom, in careers, and in communities.

A critical part of this success has been the ongoing partnership with the Los Angeles Rams. Their investment in programs like the **Watts Rams, Lincoln Rams, and Youth Leadership Council** has gone beyond financial support, and it has been a consistent commitment to showing up, providing mentorship, and opening doors that many of our youth never thought possible. By using their platform to highlight and uplift young people, the **Rams** have helped instill the belief that no dream is too big and no goal is out of reach.

The collaboration between **Project Blue**, *iPlay iLead Academy,* and the **Los Angeles Rams** is a living example of what happens when access and opportunity intersect with mentorship and belief. Sports may be the entry point, but the real win is what happens after the young people leave our programs with the skills, resilience, and a vision to succeed in life. That is the true victory: creating a pathway where dreams are nurtured, futures are built, and youth are empowered to reach their highest potential.

MAYE'S 5 KEY CHAPTER TAKEAWAYS: CHAPTER 4

1. **Sports as a Gateway, Not the Goal** – iPlay iLead Academy was founded on the idea that sports can serve as an entry point. Still, the actual mission is teaching life skills like resilience, responsibility, discipline, and leadership that prepare youth for the game of life.

2. **The Power of Intentional Design** – Every drill, reflection, and conversation was crafted to connect lessons on the court to real-world principles, turning setbacks, teamwork, and achievements into teachable moments that build character.

3. **Mentorship Unlocks Transformation** – From Kurt Rambis' involvement to partnerships with the Los Angeles Rams, the Academy's growth shows how consistent mentorship, access, and support can inspire youth to dream bigger and believe in their potential.

4. **A Whole-Child, Holistic Approach** – By integrating sports, mentorship, emotional wellness, the arts, and family engagement, iPlay iLead goes beyond athletics to nurture the mind, body, and spirit—transforming not just youth but also families and communities.

5. **Collaboration Multiplies Impact** – Through Project Blue's principles of **Convening, Elevating, Amplifying, and Communicating (CEAC)**, iPlay iLead expanded into a year-round movement, proving that united efforts create opportunities that change lives far beyond the game.

This story is about a 5th-grade young lady named Aiden. She was once a student full of energy and smiles, but during this particular time of her life, that positive energy and those smiles seemed to have faded away.

This particular day, the once-eager student found herself staring blankly at her homework, falling behind in class, and shrinking into the background. Her teachers noticed, her mom worried, and Aiden? She just felt lost. The joy she once carried into the classroom and even onto the soccer field had dimmed.

One afternoon after gym class, Coach Tee pulled Aiden aside. She wasn't just the school's P.E. teacher and soccer coach, but she was the kind of adult every student felt safe around. With gentle eyes and a listening ear, Coach Tee spent recess with Aiden and helped her open up through simple dialogue.

That moment became a turning point. She shared more than she'd ever shared before about feeling overwhelmed, confused, and like she wasn't enough. Coach Tee didn't offer instant fixes or empty words. She just provided presence.

And then, Coach Tee introduced Aiden to another influential mentor, Ms. Rene, who invited Aiden to an upcoming event. That weekend, Aiden attended a young women's empowerment program with Ms. Rene. It was a space filled with laughter, honesty, sisterhood, and stories from strong women who had walked similar paths. For the first time in a long time, Aiden didn't feel alone.

Week by week, Coach Tee became more than a coach; she became a mentor. She continued to surround Aiden with a community of women who modeled resilience, self-love, and leadership. She helped her see that mistakes didn't define her, and that giving herself grace was a kind of strength. With each passing month, Aiden's grades began to rise. But more *importantly, so did her spirit. She smiled more, she led more, and she believed more.*

This chapter is a testament to mentors like Coach Tee, who recognize that sports are just the doorway. It's the life skills, the relationships, and the emotional guidance that truly shape a child's future. When a coach becomes a mentor and teacher, they teach more than games; instead, they teach life. And sometimes, that kind of teaching changes everything.

CHAPTER 5

The Role of the Coach as Mentor & Teacher

When we talk about the power of sports, what we're really talking about is the power of people, especially coaches. Coaches have the unique opportunity to be some of the most impactful adults in a young person's life. But to fully step into that role, we must embrace a mindset shift: from simply winning games to building people. Yes, winning feels good. It's exciting, it energizes teams, and it creates moments of celebration. But if our purpose as coaches begins and ends with the scoreboard, then we're missing the bigger opportunity. A great coach is a mentor and teacher first, someone who uses the game not just to mold players, but to help shape character, discipline, resilience, and leadership. We are in the business of development, not domination. Our job isn't just to prepare youth to win the next game, but it's to help them win at life.

One of the most significant distinctions in the coaching world is when we compare major league coaches to minor league coaches. Major league coaches get paid to win. Their contracts, careers, and reputations often depend on it. But minor league coaches? Their purpose is very different as they're paid to develop players for the next level. And that's precisely the approach youth coaches must take. Our job isn't to replicate the pressure of professional sports; it's to build the foundation that gives young people a chance to reach their full athletic, emotional, and social potential.

Whether we hope to develop the next world-class athlete or simply a confident, compassionate, and goal-oriented individual, the answer is the same: player development. When done right, we help kids become champions and not just on the scoreboard, but in the way they carry themselves through life.

A popular saying tells us that "sports build character," but this statement is only partly true. Sports *can* build character, but they don't do so automatically. In fact, sports can actually harm young people when led poorly. The real power of sports lies in the quality of relationships, the climate of safety, and the culture created by the ADULTS involved.

This is why coaching with purpose, empathy, and integrity matters so deeply. Champion coaches understand this. They care more about how the game is played than whether it was won or lost. They focus on effort over talent, development over domination, and personal growth over personal glory. They know that teaching a kid to bounce back after a failure, lead with humility, or play unselfishly is far more critical than what's written in the win-loss column. These coaches give the game back to the kids, letting them take responsibility, make mistakes, and grow into leaders in the process. Now I understand that collecting wins in the Win/Loss column is part of it, and I get it, but I have a question for you: "At what expense?"

On the other hand, **ego-centered coaches** often make the game about themselves. Their self-worth becomes tied to the outcome of a game. When they win, they feel powerful. When they lose, they blame others, lash out, or shut down. These coaches turn what should be a fun, rewarding, and life-changing experience into one filled with anxiety, pressure, and burnout. And in doing so, they rob the game of its magic. That's why we must draw a line in the sand and choose to be **champion coaches**. We create cultures where expectations are clear, relationships are strong, and youth are empowered to own their experiences. When athletes feel empowered, trusted, and supported, they show up differently. They become accountable. They communicate better. They lead naturally. This is what actual development looks like.

In the end, our most incredible legacy as coaches won't be the trophies we win, but rather the lives we shape. Our job is to coach the person, not just the player. To teach lessons that live far beyond the game. And to always remember: winning might get the headlines, but developing champions both on and off the field is what truly changes the world.

The terms *Champion Coach* and *Ego-Driven Coach* come from the Play Like a Champion training program, which deeply shaped my understanding of these approaches.

Champion Coach vs Ego-Driven Coach

Champion Coach	Ego-Driven Coach
Focuses on development over domination	Focuses on winning at all costs
Sees self as a mentor and teacher first	Sees self as the center of the game
Prioritizes character, resilience, and leadership	Prioritizes self-image, reputation, and control
Creates a safe, empowering culture where youth own their experience	Creates a pressured, fear-based culture where players fear mistakes
Values effort, growth, and relationships over trophies	Values trophies and records over player well-being
Measures success by lives shaped and lessons taught	Measures success only by the scoreboard
Gives the game back to the kids	Takes the game from the kids, making it about themselves

MAYE'S 5 KEY CHAPTER TAKEAWAYS: CHAPTER 5

1. Coaches hold transformative power: The role of a coach goes far beyond teaching a sport—they are mentors and life-shapers who can guide youth in building discipline, resilience, leadership, and character.

2. Youth coaching is about development, not domination: Unlike professional coaches who are paid to win, youth coaches must focus on nurturing players' growth athletically, emotionally, and socially.

3. Sports don't automatically build character: The positive or negative impact of sports depends on the adults involved, the culture created, and the emphasis placed on effort, growth, and integrity over winning.

4. Champion coaches vs. ego-driven coaches: Champion coaches prioritize relationships, empowerment, and personal growth, while ego-driven coaches tie self-worth to wins and risk creating environments of pressure, anxiety, and burnout.

5. True coaching legacy is about people, not trophies: The greatest measure of success is not the scoreboard but the lasting impact coaches have on young people's lives—helping them become champions in life, not just in sports.

CHAPTER 6

The Power of Sports: A Practical Framework for Life Skill Integration

If we truly believe in the power of sports to shape lives, then we must treat life skill development as a core part of our coaching philosophy, not an afterthought. Just as we design practice plans to sharpen physical performance, we must be equally intentional about integrating the life skills that help young people grow into successful, well-rounded individuals. This chapter offers a practical framework that bridges the gap between athletic development and real-world readiness. It's a coaching model grounded in four essential cornerstones: Character & Accountability, Communication & Relationships, Vision & Purpose, and Resilience & Mental Toughness. When embraced consistently, these principles elevate sports from just a game to a powerful vehicle for lifelong growth.

Character & Accountability

This cornerstone emphasizes the importance of integrity, discipline, and responsibility, with qualities that extend far beyond the field. On a team, character is evident in how athletes treat their teammates, how they respond to mistakes, and how they uphold team expectations. As coaches, we can build this through Practice to Life drills that emphasize decision-making under pressure, reward hustle over highlight plays, and hold players accountable for their effort and attitude. We can ask athletes to reflect post-game not just on what they did right or wrong in competition, but who they were as teammates and leaders. Goal check-ins are also helpful, as they help players set personal conduct standards and regularly assess their follow-through.

Communication & Relationships

Sports are one of the best arenas for youth to learn how to work with others. Team dynamics naturally create opportunities for conflict resolution, active listening, empathy, and trust-building. To intentionally develop this skill set, we must embed conversations into the rhythm of our coaching. You can use team huddles, timeouts, and film sessions to discuss how players communicated during key moments. Incorporate partner drills that require verbal coordination and communication. Facilitate moments where athletes have to coach one another. During team talks, model vulnerability and openness so your athletes feel safe doing the same. When young people view communication as a tool, not a weakness, their relationships, both on and off the field, improve.

Vision & Purpose

Young athletes often need guidance to connect their day-to-day grind with a larger personal mission. The "why" behind their hard work becomes fuel for persistence, and sports can help them uncover that deeper purpose. Start by guiding athletes through weekly goal setting and vision boards. Tie each drill or game into larger life metaphors:

What does staying focused during sprints teach you about chasing goals in life? How does learning a new play mirror taking on new challenges at school or home? The more connections they make between sport and life, the more likely they are to apply their effort with purpose, not just performance.

Resilience & Mental Toughness

Every athlete will face adversity, both in sport and in life. Whether it's a tough loss, limited playing time, or personal hardship, resilience is the tool that helps them bounce back. Coaches can nurture mental toughness by intentionally incorporating adversity into practice, simulating pressure situations, and encouraging players to remain composed. After challenging moments, use post-game reflections to help them process emotions and focus on what they've learned. Reframe mistakes as necessary steps toward mastery. Celebrate comebacks, not just victories. Teach breathing techniques, visualization, and emotional regulation strategies. These tools prepare youth for the real-world challenges they'll inevitably face.

The key to this framework is integration, while making life skill development a part of everything you do, not something you add in when there's time. Whether it's a film session, a drill, a water break, or a championship game, every moment has the potential to shape who a young person becomes. The best coaches use these moments wisely. They teach, pause, challenge, and connect the dots between sport and life. When we commit to this kind of coaching, we're not just producing better athletes, but we're helping young people become stronger, wiser, and more equipped human beings.

When I teach resilience to my youth, I always reach for one simple but powerful analogy: a basketball. I hold it up in front of them and ask, "What happens when I bounce this ball on the ground while it's fully inflated?" Without hesitation, they shout, "It bounces back up!" Then I follow with, "What if I deflate it and bounce it again?" The response is just as quick: "It won't bounce, it'll stay down." That's the moment I tie it all together. I ask them to take a deep breath with me on the count of "1, 2, 3" and as they exhale, I remind them that they are like that basketball. As long as they have air in their lungs, no matter how many times life knocks them down, no matter the scars, struggles, or setbacks, they can bounce back. That breath represents life, hope, and strength. The kids light up with realization. They begin to see that their ability to rise isn't about never falling, but it's about staying full of the things that keep them going: breath, belief, and resilience. It's an analogy that sticks, not just with children, but with adults as well. It uses the language of sports to teach one of life's most important lessons: you can bounce back from anything.

MAYE'S 5 KEY CHAPTER TAKEAWAYS: CHAPTER 6

1. Life skills must be central, not secondary: Coaching should intentionally integrate life skill development—just as much as physical training—so sports become a tool for lifelong growth.

2. Four cornerstones of development: The framework rests on Character & Accountability, Communication & Relationships, Vision & Purpose, and Resilience & Mental Toughness—each designed to prepare youth for both sport and life.

3. Practical integration matters: Every moment (practice, games, huddles, even water breaks) can be used to teach lessons about teamwork, leadership, discipline, and self-reflection.

4. Resilience as a core lesson: Coaches should normalize adversity, teach coping strategies, and reframe mistakes as growth opportunities, equipping youth with the ability to bounce back stronger.

5. Powerful sports metaphors: Simple, relatable analogies (like the basketball bounce-back lesson) help athletes internalize life skills, making lessons memorable and transformative beyond the game

CHAPTER 7

Building Values, Identity, and Emotional Safety in Youth Sports Programs

The true power of sports doesn't live in wins or losses; it lives in identity. It's in the fabric of a program that stands for something. When we build youth sports programs on strong, intentional values, we create spaces that don't just train athletes; we raise human beings. Young people don't just need a field or a ball; they need a sense of belonging, structure, and adults who are willing to see them, not just their performance.

Program Identity Built on Values

Every great program starts with identity. Not just logos, chants, or uniforms, but values that serve as the moral compass for everyone involved. Programs that thrive over time are rooted in principles like respect, accountability, effort, brotherhood, discipline, compassion, and resilience. These are the building blocks that should guide every decision, every practice plan, every conversation.

And it doesn't stop with the kids. Coaches, mentors, and volunteers must also embody these values. This creates alignment, consistency, and trust. When youth know what a program stands for, it gives them something to hold on to and something to believe in.

Partnering with Families, Schools, and Communities

Too often, youth programs operate in silos, disconnected from the other critical forces in a young person's life. However, the actual impact occurs when we link arms with families, educators, and the community.

Families bring context, support, and reinforcement. They're not just spectators, they're partners.

Schools can offer valuable insights into academic struggles, behavioral patterns, and emotional needs.

Communities bring opportunities, mentorship, and safety nets that help kids thrive beyond the field.

When everyone is aligned and engaged, the program becomes part of a support system, not just an extracurricular activity.

A Rites of Passage Model

Sports programs should serve as rites of passage. Traditions, benchmarks, and meaningful moments of transition are critical for young men and women growing up in a world that often lacks intentional mentorship.

Welcome traditions for new players

Acknowledgements that normalize positivity and leadership

Acknowledgements that help kids transition to their next stage of life

Team-led chants that reinforce unity, brotherhood, and growth

These are not just events, they're formative moments that help shape character and build legacy.

Team Culture & Emotional Safety

The heartbeat of any successful program is its culture, and culture is shaped by how people feel. Do your kids feel safe? Valued? Seen? Heard? Supported?

It starts with three pillars: Trust, Belonging, and Consistency.

Trust is built through intentional relationship-building. It's choosing connection over correction.

Belonging occurs when kids know they are accepted for who they are and have a meaningful role in the team's success.

Consistency is about showing up, not just physically, but emotionally. A predictable structure and clear expectations help children feel secure.

Conflict, Cliques, and Competition

All teams face internal challenges: cliques that isolate, competition that breeds jealousy, and conflict that boils over. These can fracture a team's identity if not addressed intentionally.

Healthy competition should be fostered, not forced. Teach kids to compete with respect for themselves and their teammates. When cliques form, create intentional groupings to break them down. When conflict arises, lean into it as a teachable moment, not a reason for punishment.

Coaches should be trained in trauma-informed strategies. Kids bring more than athletic energy to practice; they bring grief, hunger, stress, fear, and pain. And when those things go unacknowledged, they show up as "attitudes," "disrespect," or "laziness."

But what they really are... are calls for help.

The Power of the Check-In

One of the most underutilized coaching tools is the check-in. It takes five seconds to ask, "How's your day?" But those five seconds can change everything.

I remember one day clearly. A kid showed up to practice thoroughly off. His body language was closed, his energy low, his face full of frustration. He struggled through drills and eventually received discipline from a coach who deemed his behavior disrespectful. The coach kept adding laps, trying to make a point, and eventually the kid snapped. He refused. He quit.

He wasn't being disrespectful. He was drowning.

After he walked off, I didn't correct him. I approached with care. I said, "It's terrific to see you today." Then, "How's your week been?"

He didn't know I had watched the whole situation unfold. He didn't expect grace. He just exhaled and finally said, "Everything has been a living hell."

Turns out, he and his family had been homeless all week. He hadn't eaten. He was hurting. And all he needed was someone to ask.

This is the essence of what we need in our programs: coaches who lead with compassion before correction. Coaches who see the kid, not just the player. Coaches who understand that an 11-year-old brain doesn't always know how to process real-life trauma, especially while running wind sprints.

We lost that kid for a moment, not because he didn't love football but because we made it about ego, not empathy.

Reclaiming Culture Through Love and Identity

When you build a program rooted in emotional safety, you shift the culture. Children begin to check in with one another. Vulnerability becomes a strength. Brotherhood becomes real. The team isn't just a roster, it's a family. And when the game is on the line, they know how to show up for each other.

More importantly, they take those lessons off the field. They show up for their families, their classmates, their future relationships, and themselves because they've been shown how.

This is how games are won. This is how life is won. This is the Power of Sports!

MAYE'S 5 KEY CHAPTER TAKEAWAYS: CHAPTER 7

1. Program identity is rooted in values, not victories: Strong programs are built on principles like respect, discipline, resilience, and compassion—shaping who kids become, not just how they play.

2. Partnerships expand impact: The most effective programs work in collaboration with families, schools, and communities, creating a comprehensive support system that nurtures youth beyond the field.

3. Sports as rites of passage: Traditions, benchmarks, and rituals help athletes feel a sense of belonging, growth, and legacy, turning sports into meaningful, life-shaping experiences.

4. Culture and emotional safety are foundational: Trust, belonging, and consistency create an environment where kids feel safe, valued, and supported—essential for both personal and athletic development.

5. Challenges must be addressed with empathy: Cliques, competition, and conflict can harm culture, but trauma-informed coaching and intentional guidance turn these into opportunities for growth and healing.

CHAPTER 8

Measuring Success Beyond the Scoreboard

Every year, so many young athletes lace up their cleats, tie their sneakers, or zip up their uniforms with dreams of fun, teamwork, and growth. But by the time many reach their early teens, those dreams have faded. In fact, research shows that one in three young people quit organized sports every year, and by age 13, a staggering 70% have abandoned the games they once loved.

Why are so many young people turning away from sports? The answer is often heartbreaking in its simplicity, but it's the toxic experiences themselves. Whether it's the pressure to win at all costs, being sidelined or screamed at by a coach, or being made to feel like performance matters more than personal growth, the competitive culture in youth sports is pushing kids out rather than lifting them. When sports programs prioritize scoreboards over self-worth and outcomes over character, the consequences are far-reaching. Young people miss out on what sports are supposed to offer, such as confidence, community, resilience, leadership, and the life lessons that stay with them long after the final whistle blows.

By no means am I saying that we shouldn't train hard or avoid those adverse moments; I am simply saying that we need to strike a balance, and right now the balance is tipping heavily in the wrong direction.

This chapter challenges the outdated belief that success in youth athletics can be measured solely by wins and losses. Instead, let's explore how the most impactful sports programs focus on developing the whole person physically, emotionally, socially, and mentally. At our organization, we've reimagined what success looks like. Yes, we still play hard. Yes, we still celebrate victories. But more importantly, we track what really matters, which is the kind of growth that doesn't show up on the scoreboard. In our programs, success is defined by the life outcomes of our youth, not just their athletic performance.

We monitor the academic progress of participants, including:

- GPA increases and grade stability are measured through grade-level-based evaluation in reading, writing, mathematics, and science.
- Engagement in tutoring and enrichment programs

In the last 12 months, 83% of participants improved or maintained a 2.5 GPA or higher, after being connected with our academic support services.

We partnered with an independent agency to conduct self-assessments and receive feedback from our youth, parents, and mentors to measure growth in:

- Self-confidence
- Emotional Well-being
- Self-efficacy

After six months in our programs, 78% of youth participants reported feeling "more confident" in school, at home, and on the field.

Our coaches and mentors complete regular check-ins to track:

- Peer-to-peer relationships
- Leadership traits and accountability
- Emotional regulation and response to adversity

Youth who participate in both our sports and life skills programs show an 83% increase in positive peer interactions and teamwork behaviors.

One of our most powerful success indicators is the building of strong relationships. Every young athlete in our programs is connected to at least one consistent adult mentor who invests in their life beyond practice. Through regular surveys and touchpoints:

- 80% of our youth say they have an adult mentor they trust.
- 100% say they now see themselves as future leaders in their schools or communities.

These results don't come from just showing up and running drills. They come from coaches who are also mentors, teachers, and individuals who see youth sports as a platform for life transformation. We partner with different partners to train our staff to focus on:

- Child Development
- Emotional safety
- Positive reinforcement
- Character-based leadership

- Team building and reflection time after every practice or game
- Mentorship

If we want youth sports to be a force for good, we must ask ourselves new questions, such as:

- Did the young athlete walk away more confident than they arrived?
- Did they learn how to lead, even in a loss?
- Did they feel loved, seen, and heard by the adults guiding them?
- Did they develop the courage to try again, fail again, and grow again?

This is what matters, and this mindset is how we should present ourselves to our youth. Kobe Bryant once said, "Sports is the greatest metaphor we have for life." If this is to be true, then we must hold ourselves accountable for how we show up for our youth and how we define success. The micro game may be basketball, but the macro game is life.

MAYE'S 5 KEY CHAPTER
TAKEAWAYS: CHAPTER 8

1. Youth are leaving sports at alarming rates — 70% quit by age 13, often due to toxic experiences like pressure to win, lack of playing time, or negative coaching that prioritizes outcomes over personal growth.

2. True success extends beyond the scoreboard — the most impactful programs measure growth in physical, emotional, social, and mental aspects, not just wins and losses.

3. Academic progress is part of athletic success — structured support, such as tutoring and enrichment, helps youth improve or maintain their GPA, demonstrating the value of blending sports with education.

4. Mentorship and relationships are powerful drivers — consistent connections with caring adults help youth build trust, confidence, leadership, and resilience that extend beyond sports.

5. Coaches must be mentors, not just trainers — by focusing on child development, emotional safety, and character-based leadership, coaches help athletes walk away more confident, connected, and prepared for life.

It was early in the season, still warm enough that practice ended with kids dripping in sweat and gulping water as if it were gold. We had a solid group that year: a mix of returning players, a handful of first-year kids finding their footing, and a staff of committed coaches, many of whom were also dads. That wasn't new for us. We'd worked hard over the years to establish a team culture where coaching and parenting could coexist respectfully and effectively. But that season, one story stood out.

Coach Mike was new to our staff, who was a seasoned football mind, a great communicator, and was immediately well-respected by players and coaches alike. He was positive, passionate, and had that rare ability to make the game fun without lowering the standard. The kids responded to him almost instantly. All but one. That one was his son, Jay.

Now, if you'd seen them off the field, you'd swear they were best friends. Jay lit up around his dad. They worked out together at the park, they posted funny videos after practice, and they laughed in the car. It was clear they had a real bond. But on the field, something changed.

When Jay made a mistake, Coach Mike became a completely different person. The tone got sharper, the corrections louder, the frustration more intense. He wasn't just coaching anymore, but he was unloading. While he praised and uplifted the other kids, he treated Jay like a soldier in boot camp. And Jay, who was one of our most talented players, would shut down every time it happened. Shoulders slumped, eye contact gone, and energy drained. From that moment forward, he was no longer productive in practice. This didn't happen once, but it happened repeatedly.

One day after a particularly tough session, one of our veteran coaches pulled me aside. "We need to talk," he said. And just like that, a staff meeting was set for that evening.

We didn't name names, nor did we point fingers. We revisited our coaching philosophy to reaffirm why we do this, who we do it for, and the *importance of protecting the mental and emotional development of all our players. I shared a story from a few years back about a similar situation with another parent-coach, and the fallout that came from not recognizing the difference between coaching your child and raising your child. Then I asked each of our coaches to reflect on when they were 12, 13, or 14 years old, still learning the game and unsure of themselves.*

"How would you have responded," I asked, "if the person you looked up to most came down on you the hardest every time you messed up?" It got quiet in that room. We left that meeting aligned. Everyone. Including Coach Mike. No one had to say his name, but we all knew the real-life story behind the message.

Fast forward a few weeks. It's mid-season, and we're playing one of the toughest teams in our division. It's close. Every drive matters. Then, a blown assignment. And it came from Jay.

I saw Coach Mike's face go red. I could feel the heat from across the field. The whole staff braced for what we expected to come, which was another explosion. This was Coach Mike's defensive unit, which was his responsibility, and it was his son who made the big mistake. But then, something amazing happened.

Coach Mike took a breath. He pulled Jay aside, but not in front of the whole team, not with fire in his eyes, but with poise, and he corrected him. Yes, he held him accountable, but this time, he spoke with belief. He reminded Jay of who he was. He treated him not like his son, but like an athlete, just like the rest. You could see Jay come back to life, and just a few plays later, he made the game-sealing interception.

The team exploded. The sidelines went wild. And right there, in the middle of it all, Coach Mike grabbed Jay in a bear hug, not as his dad, but as his coach. It was pure and it was right. It was exactly what we want youth sports to be. That moment stuck with all of us. It was a win on the scoreboard, sure, but more importantly, it was a win in how we coach, how we parent, and how we love.

Coach Mike learned to coach his son up, not coach him down. He realized that holding your child to a high standard doesn't require breaking their spirit. And when he made that shift, Jay didn't just play better, but he grew. In that moment, the team won, the coach won, and more than anyone, the kid won.

CHAPTER 9

The Dual Role: Parenting and Coaching

In the world of youth sports, few dynamics are more complex and more critical to get right than that of a parent serving as a coach. It's a position of great opportunity, but also great responsibility. When done right, it can be a powerful and transformative experience for both the parent and the child. However, when blurred lines go unchecked, it can create confusion, damage relationships, and even erode a young athlete's love for the game.

The Line Between Coach and Parent

The first and most important truth for any parent-coach to understand is this: you must separate your role as a parent from your role as a coach.

This is not just about titles; it's about mindset, language, tone, and approach. When a child is on the field, court, or track, they are one of many players and are part of a team. As their coach, your job is to develop, guide, correct, and lead them in the same way you would any other athlete on the team. The moment a parent begins treating their child differently, either with favoritism or with an excessive standard, they compromise the integrity of their role and create confusion in a young mind that's still trying to understand identity, performance, and belonging.

Children may not always be able to articulate this confusion, but they feel it. One moment, the person driving them to practice is a nurturing parent who offers support and snacks. The next, that same person is yelling from the sidelines or breaking down game film with a tone that feels far more critical than constructive. This seesaw of roles can leave a child emotionally disoriented, especially if there's no clear boundary between when the coaching stops and the parenting begins.

Accountability Must Be Universal

Yes, parent-coaches must hold their children accountable. But that accountability must be no different than what's expected from every other player on the team. If you demand discipline, effort, and execution from your child, then demand it from every child. That fairness is what builds trust not only with your child but with their teammates and your coaching staff.

Often, parent-coaches fall into one of two traps. The first is giving their child special treatment, such as extra playtime, fewer consequences, or overpraise. The second is going too far in the opposite direction, being harder on their child than anyone else out of fear of appearing biased. Neither approach is healthy.

If a coach is too harsh with their own child, thinking it's a way to "toughen them up" or "set an example," it can lead to emotional shutdown. Once that happens, the child stops listening, stops learning, and begins resenting not only the game but also the parent. And now the team has lost a contributor, the coach has lost effectiveness, and the parent-child relationship becomes strained, all in the name of accountability.

Knowing What Your Child Can Handle

This conversation becomes even more complex when we factor in life skills. Yes, sports are about more than wins and losses as they're about resilience, overcoming adversity, and dealing with pressure. But every child is different. Some individuals thrive under direct criticism, while others shut down. Some rise when pushed; others fall when pressed too hard.

As a parent-coach, it is your job to know your child and what motivates them, what shuts them down, and what helps them grow. You may think you're preparing them for adversity, but if you push past their capacity, you're not teaching them to overcome; you're teaching them to withdraw. Such emotional scarring can have long-term consequences, both on and off the field.

Too many young athletes have walked away from sports, not because they didn't love the game, but because they couldn't handle the emotional pressure of being coached by someone they couldn't escape from when the game was over. They grew resentment, not resilience.

Letting Other Coaches Do Their Job

One of the most disruptive habits a parent-coach can develop is shielding their child from the influence and instruction of other coaches. Every good team has multiple voices, and every athlete benefits from hearing things in different ways. If a fellow coach offers correction, feedback, or direction to your child, that should be welcomed, not resented.

The moment you say, *"No one talks to my child like that but me,"* you have ceased to be a coach; you have returned to being a parent in the wrong moment. Unless that correction is disrespectful or inappropriate, it is your job to support the other coaches and allow them to do what they've been entrusted to do. Undermining a coach's authority in front of the team does not protect your child; it isolates them, damages staff unity, and can break down the team culture you're trying to build. Coaching is a team effort. That means everyone on the staff has a voice, and your child needs to hear them all.

Coaching All Kids Like They're Yours

Here's the beauty of getting this dynamic right: when a parent fully embraces the role of coach, they begin to coach every kid as if they were their own. They hold them to high standards, correct with love, teach with patience, and pour belief into each player. When this happens, something powerful shifts. You're no longer just your child's parent, but you've become a mentor and a role model to many. That's when parent-coaches become some of the most beloved and impactful leaders in youth sports. Every child on that team deserves the same level of respect, investment, and attention. When you wear the coaching hat, you are a parent to all. Well, at least for that hour, that practice, that season.

Parents as Spectators: Staying in Your Lane

Let's shift the lens now to another crucial role: parents as spectators. Too often, we see games where parents are coaching from the stands by shouting instructions, correcting their kids mid-play, or giving directions that directly contradict what the coach has asked the team to do. This not only confuses the child, but it chips away at the trust between the coach and the athlete.

Imagine being a young player who has spent an entire week listening, learning, and executing their coach's instructions, only to hear their parent yelling something totally different from the stands. Now the child is torn. Do they follow their coach? Or do they obey their parent, someone they love, respect, and probably fear disappointing? That tension doesn't just stay on the field. It follows them home, weighing on their confidence and eroding their ability to be fully present in the game.

Parents, this is not your moment to coach. It's your moment to support.

When you coach from the stands, you not only confuse your child, but you also create division between yourself and the coach, and by extension, your child and their team. Over time, this undermines the coach's authority and can fracture the entire team dynamic.

Instead of shouting out directions, try shouting out encouragement. Teach your child that once the game starts, it's the coach's voice they must trust. Support the coach publicly even if you don't always agree privately. That unity teaches your child to respect leadership, trust a process, and operate within a system, which are skills that translate well beyond the game.

Final Thoughts

Being a parent-coach is not easy, but it can be one of the most rewarding roles you'll ever take on, if you do it with clarity, humility, and consistency. Understand when to wear the coaching hat and when to step back into your parenting role. Let others coach your child. Respect the voices around you. And when you're watching from the stands, be the supporter your child needs, not the second coach they didn't ask for.

Above all, remember this: sports should be a gift, a place where young people fall in love with the game, build life-long friendships, learn who they are, and discover what they're capable of. When adults, whether coaching or watching, understand their role, the game remains pure, the lessons remain strong, and the love for the sport stays alive. And that is the true power of sports.

MAYE'S 5 KEY CHAPTER TAKEAWAYS: CHAPTER 9

1. Separate the roles of parent and coach: Clear boundaries are essential—favoritism or harsher treatment of your own child can cause confusion, emotional strain, and damage both the team and the parent-child relationship.

2. Accountability must be fair and consistent: Parent-coaches should hold their child to the same standards as every other player, avoiding both special treatment and excessive criticism.

3. Know your child's emotional capacity: Every child responds differently to pressure and correction; pushing too hard can cause resentment and withdrawal rather than resilience and growth.

4. Support other coaches and staff: Undermining teammates' authority or shielding your child from correction disrupts team unity; coaching should be collaborative, with every player benefiting from multiple voices.

5. Parents as spectators must encourage, not coach. Shouting instructions from the stands can cause confusion and undermine trust; parents should model support, unity, and respect for leadership.

PART III

Voices from the Field

CHAPTER 10

Youth Perspectives

Shaun Thomas Interview:

My name is Shaun Thomas Jr. I attend Verbum Dei Jesuit High School, and I'm going to the 11th grade. I've been a part of the iPlay-iLead Academy for four years.

How would you describe the experience?

The experience at iPlayiLead has been great for me, and it's an overall excellent program for young people. For example, if you are growing up as a kid and don't have programs like this, this is a good way to start. You know, you get to learn new things, not only just sports, but also, you know, life skills

When you hear, you know, I play, I lead, like, what does that mean by the title? What does the title mean to you? And how do you see the title reflecting the things we do out there?

When I hear 'iPlay,' I think of how people incorporate actions into their lives. So, for example, for me, whenever I'm, you know, playing sports, I think of, you know, how can I, you know, do this thing and how can I put my actions into play? And then, when I hear 'iLead,' I think of how people are leaders in our society. And I think of myself and how I'm a leader of my younger siblings and also my cousins, because I'm the oldest sibling in the house. So, I would have to be like the one to protect my brother whenever my mom's not there.

Can you think about a time when something a coach here at iPlayiLead taught you during this program, but something that you had to apply outside of this field or outside of the court?
A time that I can think of when a coach actually taught me those things is I remember a couple weeks ago, I end up learning something from you, and it was just about trust in others and how to like, you know, collaborate with others because I, you know, I tend to struggle sometimes with trust in others because I don't know them or I know them issues that I have like, you know, a trust issue with people that I usually do, you know, don't hang out with all the time. I learned from you how to collaborate with others and connect with them. That way, we could either be part of something in the future or become better people and individuals in the end.

However, people must earn your trust, as it doesn't just come easily. What are the ways that the coaches here have earned your trust, you know, for you to be able to listen to them imply the things that they tell you here on the basketball court in your life?
I'll say a way that they were able to gain my trust is just by getting to know me for the past years because I use, I hope you don't mind, me using you, for example, when I first met you, I don't know if you thought it in your head, but you probably had to, you know, gain my

trust before you got to involve me with so many other things and so many other activities throughout the program, and also it goes for all the other coaches here, coach Justin and coach John, every other coach that, you know, comes to the program and volunteers here, they all have to gain my trust, and that goes for every young individual here. They all have to just like, you know, like I said, learn from their perspective because at the end of the day, you have to, you know, everyone has to leave this place, learn something.

And if they didn't, you know, then obviously a coach didn't, you know, do their job and try to teach that young individual or something. But at the end of the day, like I said, you have to leave this place learning something and, you know, even talk to a family member about it and just saying like, you know, this program is a good space for me. That's one of the reasons I like coming here, because it's a place where I feel more comfortable being myself and being free, unlike at home or school.

Shaun, can you think of a life skill that you've learned here at the program that you see yourself using, you know, outside of your everyday life?

A life skill that I learned from this program and use in my everyday life is effective communication. When I was at my school, we also participated in a corporate work-study program at CWSP. We visit various business establishments and jobs that we have to do for our tuition, not for our education. And sometimes we get gift cards for it, but that just doesn't all come to you. It's something behind that.

So, what I learned is the importance of communication with others. For my freshman year, that was my first year in high school, and I wasn't yet out of the middle school mindset. At the time, I wasn't just not communicating with people, but I also didn't know how to communicate with somebody who wasn't more professional than I was. So, I had to learn that from the programming activity we did for the younger man's program. I just have to learn and practice effective communication.

For example, I used to look at myself in the mirror and talk to myself constantly, pretending I was talking to someone else. But also, I remember the words you said that one time, look at the man and the mirror, because not everybody can just be me. I'm myself. I have to communicate with myself sometimes, get things off my chest whenever I need to.

How do you feel about just the coaches here? Do you feel like the coaches value you? Do you feel like they love you? What do you think about the coaches here?

The coaches show a lot of respect, and they value me. I also feel like they see themselves in me, because I think of my parents whenever I'm here with them and remember our earlier conversations.

Today, we had a conversation about how coaches, like those here or in general, treat players. If they don't, it's often because they don't like the player or the player has done something wrong. Still, they also don't like it; it's other to them, like not liking the player.

I just think of it as, you know, love, showing love because I remember, you would end up saying us to us earlier, if a coach or an adult is like not saying anything to you, you, they know it's wrong, then they're just like, you know, that means they don't care. But if they're showing you something that they know is wrong, they're trying to point it out to you; don't get stressed about it. That's just them showing their love to you.

Daryl Jamerson Interview:

I'm Daryl Jamison, but people call me DJ. I'm 13 years old and I'm in the 7th grade. I've been part of the program since I was 7 years old.

So, you've been part of the program since its inception. What do you like about the iPlayiLead Academy that has kept you coming back since you were 7 years old to now, at 13?

First, when I was six, I loved playing basketball. Yeah. But then the program started getting older and adding more people, and I noticed there was more importance in things like than just playing basketball. There's leadership, there's discipline. And some mistakes happen, which I've learned you still have to bounce back from. So, I've learned a great deal. My favorite is leadership, though.

Nice, I love that. It sounds like you're describing that you've learned some key transferable skills that show up in life rather than just in sports. Why is that important to you?

Because some people don't realize that certain things can be both enjoyable and educational, teaching valuable life lessons, it is essential. Like basketball! Basketball is fun. People play basketball because they love the game, but also because it is a discipline that fosters leadership. You learn from your mistakes. And if we're not learning them in basketball, then we're not wasting time; we're just playing basketball.

I love that. So, you talked about three different life skills. You spoke of leadership, discipline, and overcoming mistakes. If you had to think of a life skill that you've learned here that's showing up in your life now besides those three, what would you say?

Resilience! Resilience!

What is Resilience, and what does resilience mean to you?

To me, it means, like, bouncing back from, like, um, how do I say? Bouncing back from, like, the mistakes that happen in life. And, like, I've grown in this program because when I was younger, I used to just come here. I used to just come here to play basketball & hang out with my new friends. But now I come here to learn more about myself and discipline myself to do more than what I used to do when I was young. I've just learned a lot of new things. I'm just super grateful.

Do you feel like your peers are catching on to that stuff, too?

Yes.

Are your conversations different? If so, how so?

When you come here, we play basketball, you play football, and you do all these things, but our conversations are a little bit deeper than just the X's and O's of the sports. We discuss life, including our accomplishments and failures. We also help each other overcome our failures, and this program is massive on celebrating our accomplishments just by acknowledging them.

I want to speak about failures because you mentioned being resilient, and you described resilience as bouncing back from disappointments, hardships, and other challenges. How do you handle failures, and what has this program taught you about how to handle those failures that we all have?

Well, for me, I pray. Okay. I ask God to help me bounce back from that because I feel like it's essential for me. Additionally, you have helped me a lot by teaching me new concepts of life, and that will benefit me because it will motivate me to do more than I've done before.

I love that, and thank you for mentioning me, but you also have some other mentors here. You have Miss Tray, you have Yaya, Coach Clay, and more. Do you feel like they really love you? Why do you feel like the mentors and coaches here adore you?

I think Miss Tray really helped me because, first of all, she got me a photo shoot, and that stuff cost a lot for me. I will give her a shout-out for that. I love Miss Tray. She's like a second mom to me. She teaches me how to love myself, no matter what, and keep going, no matter the hardships. Also, yeah, I love Yaya. She's so sweet. I love Coach Clay. She used to teach me how to play basketball.

But yeah, I still keep a lot of life skills that Miss Tray and Coach Clay, you, and everybody that's taught me because, like, it's still, it's just been in my mind because whenever, like, I'm thinking of doing something that I'm not supposed to do, it goes in my mind. I stopped, and I thought, 'Let me not do that, because I feel like people who have taught me the new concept of what I'm supposed to do, rather than when I'm not supposed to, wouldn't want me to do that.' And they wouldn't be proud of me for doing that. So I feel like, yeah.

Tristian Eurin Interview:

I'm Tristian Eurin. I'm 12 years old and I'm in the 7th grade. I've been part of the program since I was in the 4th grade.

Tristan, can you think of or share a time when a coach here taught you something that you had to use outside of basketball?

In one session, you taught me about responsibility & accountability, and when I did something wrong, I told my mom that I was wrong.

I also recall learning about responsibility, where we discussed the importance of starting our day with good habits. And I think it was a time when we talked about just like how we wake up and the things that we do in the morning kind of set the tone for the rest of the day, to be disciplined. I also learned that that is the way we should approach everything, from sports to school to life.

It reminds you to have discipline. Would you say that?
Yeah, it also made me feel good.

Did it make you feel good? Why?
Because I have control over it, and that is something I apply to everything I do. Control the controllables

I love that. When you're involved in sports, we strive to teach you life skills here at the iPlayiLead Academy. And with those life skills, what would you say we try to do with those life skills that we learn in sports?
Apply them to life. We learn them to be transferable skills.

What's one transferable skill that you would say you learned here at iPlayiLead Academy that's helping you in life?
To keep trying and never give up.

And what do you mean exactly? Give me an example.
Sometimes, I don't get the drill, so I ask questions and keep trying. And like, how in life, if it knocks you down, you can bounce back up.

Nice! What do we call that to be what?

Resilience! We are all taught to be resilient people

Do you like the coaches here at iPlayiLead Academy?

I like all of them.

What is it about all of them that you like? Because obviously, you've come here to play basketball, and you have different coaches with different personalities. So, what is it about the coaches that you like? How do they make you feel?

They really care about me. They really care about all of us here

Why would you say that?

Because they like, get on us, but not in a mean way. They care about us. Some coaches don't care and let you do it, but you all care and point out our mistakes, then teach us the right way to do something in a rewarding manner.

You have a little brother who's part of the program, who's five now or something like that. But when he first started the program, he was two or something.

Yes, that is right.

How does it feel watching him grow and now become a regular participant?

It's like really cool.

I remember when he was 2, he would go around with his toys, and now he's in the drills, doing the drills just like you and the rest of the team. How do you feel about that in terms of your leadership role and leading by example for him?

I love that I get to teach him some of the drills and hopefully teach him to be better tha   n me.

Malia Sawyer Interview:

My name is Malia Sawyer. I'm finishing the ninth grade and will be entering the 10th grade. I attend St. Mary's Academy.

What sports are you playing?

I play all sports!

What would you say you learned at the iPlayiLead Academy?

It taught me to overcome some of the difficulties I had faced in life.

In life? But aren't we here for sports?

Yes, but the way I see it now, being part of this program means that sports have to connect with your mental well-being. We call them transferable skills.

Yes, I love that, Malia! Can you think of a time when a coach here has taught you something that you had to use outside of here?

Well, I will say you because you taught me how to like, when I'm angry, how to control it, my anxiety, how to prevent it.

**And what are some of the things that you do
to control that anxiety or that anger?**

I play sports to clear my mind, and I also practice breathing exercises. The breathing exercises help me because I sometimes need to stop and take a breath. Especially when I'm in those heated moments. I learn to hit the reset button, reflect, and do the right things, right!

**Would you say you used that here when
you're playing a game of sports, too?**

Yes, I get angry in sports sometimes, and the breathing helps me

**Does that help you when you get angry
at your little brother, too?**

Yes (haha), the breathing helps me the same way.

**Our main goal with this program is to use sports to teach life
skills. What's the life skill that you say that you've learned
here at iPlayiLead Academy that you had to use in life?**

To stay confident!

Why is confidence so necessary in sports and in life?

Because I feel like if you don't have confidence, then you're limited. You won't have that boost you need in life.

But how do you stay confident & how do you build confidence?

Sometimes I pray, and at other times, I talk to my coaches, who believe in me and help me believe in myself when I'm in doubt. I also practice a lot, so that helps me know I can do things because I see myself doing them when no one else is around. Then I apply that to life outside of sports, and it helps me understand that doing things repeatedly helps me become better, which in turn gives me the confidence I need.

Do you feel like the coaches here care about you?
Yes.

Why do you say so?
Because when I make mistakes, they help me. Other coaches have just let me fail and don't help, but here, they help you, and if you don't understand something, they explain it in ways that make me feel good about myself.

If you had to give some advice to any young person or any coach or mentor out there, what would you say to them?
Don't give up on your dreams and keep going.

Love that, thank you, Malia! I wish you nothing but success in high school, especially in your participation in all the sports.

Destiny Avelar Interview:

I'm Destiny Avelar, I'm 20 years old, and I'm a former participant and now Jr. Coach for the iPlayiLead Academy

You're coaching kids now and giving back after coaches poured into you. How does that make you feel?
I think it's a great community to be in, honestly. I see familiar faces I've known for years, and I get to pass along what I've learned.

Thinking back, whether when you were a participant or now as a coach, can you remember something a coach taught you that's shown up in your life outside of sports?

For sure. I've always had trouble resolving conflict. Back in grade school, you always had my back and taught me how to work things out with my teammates. How to handle and resolve conflict.

So, you're saying you approach conflict differently now?

Yeah, for sure. I focus on fixing things and doing what's right.

Do you think the same skills you use outside of sports came from playing sports?

Oh yeah, definitely. Collaboration is one, and also taking leadership. I've learned to step into leadership roles and get out of my comfort zone.

You were shy at one point, right?

Yeah, very shy.

And now you're the complete opposite. That's amazing. Leadership seems like a big takeaway for you. Is that the primary life skill you've carried into your everyday life?

Yeah, for sure. I used to follow others, but sports taught me how to take control of my own life. I want to pass that on to the next generation.

What does being a leader mean to you?

Honestly, it's about doing what you do, showing up for others, and helping them.

You do a great job at that. I remember you as one of the elite athletes, and now you're giving back not only with your basketball skills but also your mindset. When you think about your coaches back then, how did they make you feel, and how do you want your players to feel?

All the coaches here always welcomed me, asked how I was doing. That gave me an excellent feeling, and I try to do the same for the kids, checking in with them and communicating well.

Why is checking in with them so powerful?

I think it's important because sometimes I want people to ask me how I am. And with the kids, I like talking to them, especially the little ones.

And sometimes you find out their day is about more than basketball, right?

Exactly.

So, from being a participant in iPlayiLead back in grade school to now coaching here, what's one thing sports have taught you about life?

Discipline, for sure. I initially had issues with it, but staying consistent really helped me.

And now you pass that lesson on to the kids?

Yeah, discipline and consistency.

I love that. In sports and in life, if you're not disciplined or consistent, you can't be successful. Thanks, Destiny, I appreciate you.

CHAPTER 11

Coaches, Mentors, and Educators in Action

Brian Seaton (Next Level Performance Founder/Head Coach)

Coaching for life is deeply important to me because I've seen firsthand how sports shaped my own journey. My goal is to inspire young athletes to chase their dreams—not just for success on the court or field, but because the pursuit itself builds skills that last a lifetime. Sports remain one of the most powerful tools we have to teach essential life lessons. Young people who play sports learn how to collaborate, navigate adversity, and thrive under pressure — traits that prepare them not just for competition, but for life itself.

Jamal Adams (Loyola High School, Former Head Basketball Coach & Current Loyola High School President)

As a leader, I firmly believe that true success stems from assembling a team of talented individuals, establishing clear goals and benchmarks, and fostering a collaborative vision that is ambitious and driven. I am committed to creating an environment that encourages trial and error, as it is through embracing creativity that breakthroughs are made.

When faced with roadblocks and setbacks, I view them as valuable learning opportunities that enable us to grow and improve. Moreover, I recognize the significance of celebrating our achievements and leveraging them as stepping stones toward further progress. In pursuing goals, we will approach each endeavor with unwavering enthusiasm, a sense of purpose, deep respect for one another, and a shared spirit of joy.

Coach Lester Bodiford (LAPD Officer/ Watts Rams Coach/Mentor)

The relationship between a coach and a player is like no other. For most young men and women, it's the first time they put their trust into an adult that they're not related to. I consider myself a surrogate father to these kids. I pray that one day something Coach Les told them or showed them, created a spark that became a flame to ignite their passion and to be more. I coach for life because someone coached me for life to save me.

Sports are a great tool. It allows the coach to gain trust from the youth and create relationships that last a lifetime, as we all came together for a common goal that we could only achieve if we all met our full potential. For me, football, in particular, is a perfect representation of real life. All lessons about adversity, resilience, hard work, accountability, leadership, responsibility, respect, fear, wins, and losses — they all help form a great human. What you learn in the field, you can apply off the field.

Coach Jen Aveda (CSUDH Women's Volleyball Coach)

After 25 years of coaching women's college volleyball from an assistant to a head coach and coaching club/youth along the way, stepping away from the court has not distanced me from the lessons, relationships, or purpose that coaching brought into my life. If anything, it has sharpened my view of what matters most—and why we must continue to fight for sports as more than just a game.

Coaching is more than the wins and losses, although at the college level, it does play a significant role in the livelihood of your career. What I do know, and what my past players have come to find out as well, is that wins and losses fade with time. What endures are the people—the young women who walked into the gym unsure of their strength, their voice, or their worth, and left with a better sense of all three.

For me, "coaching for life" means being intentional about shaping character, not just performance. It's the way we talk about failure after a tough loss. It's the way we push through discomfort in conditioning to discover resilience. It's the team meeting that turns into a life conversation. It holds high standards—not only on the court, but also in the classroom, in relationships, and in personal growth.

But more than anything, coaching for life is about relationships. Some of the strongest, most meaningful connections I've made have come through the shared journey of sport. I've watched teammates become lifelong friends, roommates, bridesmaids, and business partners. I've been invited to weddings, baby showers, and milestone moments years after athletes have graduated. The bond forged through sweat, trust, failure, laughter, and belief—those relationships don't end when the season does. They last a lifetime.

I've seen athletes become leaders, not just because they could jump higher or hit harder, but because they learned how to communicate effectively, take responsibility, and uplift others. That transformation—that shift from player to empowered person—is why coaching for life matters.

Sports are a mirror. They reflect who we are under pressure, and they push us to confront what we're made of. For young people—especially today—sports offer one of the last truly immersive, real-time training grounds for life.

Where else do you learn to fail publicly and bounce back? Where else are you asked to give everything for something bigger than yourself, even when no one is watching? Where else do you meet mentors who hold you accountable and believe in you all at once?

In a world of constant distraction, social pressure, and individualism, sports call young people into focus, discipline, humility, and community. That's rare, and that's worth protecting.

We must continue fighting for this space—not just for the elite or the gifted, but for every young person who needs to know they are capable of accomplishing complex things. That their voice matters. That leadership isn't about status but service.

I may not be coaching on the sidelines anymore, but I'll always be a coach at heart. Because the actual scoreboard isn't measured in awards, banners, medals, and trophies—it's in the lives touched, the confidence built, and the people who leave better than they arrived.

That's why I coached. And that's why I believe we must continue to use sport as a vehicle for growth, connection, and life.

Coach Justin Rhone (iPlayiLead Academy Coach)

Life coaching matters because it helps people, young and old, unlock potential they never knew they had, and to live with a greater purpose, clarity, and resilience. More so important in young people because it helps provide the structure, guidance, and empowerment we all need at a very crucial period of growth and decision-making.

Using sports to reach young people is powerful because it teaches life lessons that extend outside of the basketball court. We can emphasize that it's not only about what it takes to win on the court, but also about what it takes to win off the court. It helps to build character, confidence, and creates far-reaching opportunities. It's simple: take the thing young people enjoy the most, want to be the best at, will show up to every day, and layer it with life skills.

Coach DeMira Pierra (Women's Youth Basketball Coach)

Coaching for life matters to me because I believe that life is a sport. To win, you have to be equipped with the tools of perseverance, discipline, and patience. These are all characteristics of a champion. We just don't want to compete in life; we want to show up and become champions of life!

Sports provide a safe space for children to explore new interests, build identity, and apply life lessons that will serve them as they continue to grow. With that being said, a coach helps create a healthy village for children to feel seen, heard, and valued, which directly impacts their self-esteem.

Coach Robert Garcia (Watts Rams Head Coach)

Why does coaching for life matter to me? It matters because as a young child I loved sports. Sports were my outlet from my home and everyday life. I had some good coaches and some not-so-great. I realized that as I got older, I wanted to help young boys like me. To help mold them into great men, be someone they could look up to and support.

The reason we must continue sports is that some of the children where I'm from have anger issues, come from single-parent households, or have low incomes. These sports help them escape their situations temporarily, meet new people outside of their communities, and expose them to things they have never seen or done. They build character and discipline, which every child needs.

Coach/Veteran Educator Yanick Clay (iPlayiLead Academy)

For young women living in inner-city neighborhoods or growing up in poverty, access to opportunity can be limited by systemic inequality, underfunded schools, and a lack of resources. Yet, in these challenging environments, sports—when paired with good coaching—can be a powerful pathway to personal growth, social mobility, and emotional well-being. Coaching in sports becomes more than just about winning games; it becomes a source of structure, empowerment, and hope for young women navigating the challenges of low socioeconomic conditions.

Good coaching provides stability and support where it may be otherwise lacking. In many low-income households, economic hardship can lead to instability and a lack of adult role models. A dedicated coach offers consistency—someone who shows up, listens, guides, and believes in the potential of each player. For young women, especially those who often face additional challenges such as gender bias, safety concerns, or caring for siblings at a young age, a coach can be a crucial mentor. This relationship fosters a safe space where girls feel valued and heard, which is essential for their emotional development and self-worth.

Socially, participation in sports builds community and a sense of belonging, which is especially important in areas where youth may feel isolated or marginalized. A good coach fosters teamwork, respect, and accountability. These lessons help young women form positive relationships with peers and adults, improving their communication and conflict resolution skills. Coaches who promote inclusion, discipline, and mutual respect help young athletes avoid negative social influences, such as gangs or toxic environments, which can be common in underserved communities.

Educationally, intense coaching can be a gateway to academic achievement. Coaches often set high expectations not just on the field, but in the classroom. They monitor grades, offer encouragement, and connect players to tutoring or college prep programs. Many young women from low-income backgrounds are first-generation college students, and coaches can be instrumental in helping them believe that college is possible. Athletic scholarships and access to higher education may become attainable through sports, but even without scholarships, the discipline and time management skills gained through athletics support academic success.

Economically, sports can lead to long-term career opportunities. While only a few athletes go on to play professionally, many young women who are exposed to sports develop skills that employers value, including leadership, perseverance, goal-setting, and teamwork. Coaches can open doors to internships, job references, or connections to community programs that support career development. Furthermore, female athletes often gain the confidence to pursue fields traditionally dominated by men, including business, law, and public service.

Emotionally, sports provide an outlet for stress, trauma, and anxiety—everyday experiences in under-resourced neighborhoods. Good coaches teach resilience, self-regulation, and how to bounce back from failure. These coping skills are essential for young women facing adversity. Through positive reinforcement, goal-setting, and encouragement, coaches help girls believe in their own strength and take pride in their progress, both on and off the field.

In conclusion, for young women in low-income communities, good coaching in sports can be life-changing. It's not just about athletic achievement—it's about unlocking potential, building confidence, and creating real opportunities for a better future.

Coach Monique Adams (LA Legends Founder and Head Coach)

Coaching for life matters to me because I see the void it fills for our young athletes. The need for coaching and validation is often overlooked in our young athletes, and we must continue to guide them in areas that aren't showcased on a video screen or in a text message. What it looks like to show up every day, what it looks like to believe in someone, and what it looks like to be a part of a team that relies on you.

Using sports as a tool enables us as coaches to reach them in numerous ways. From building character to developing mental toughness, battling adversity, and handling wins and losses in the best way, these skills will continue to prepare them for the next game or chapter in life. Sports are a vessel that encompasses many skills needed throughout life and provides opportunities to build confidence and face challenges head-on.

Renata Simril (President & CEO, LA84 Foundation)

"Sports and coaching matter to me because they are a gateway to possibility. Well-trained and caring coaches meet kids where they are and create safe spaces for kids to try without judgment. They teach discipline, resilience, confidence, and connection—and when done right, they build not just athletes, but citizens, leaders, and whole human beings. That's why the work Marc May leads through Project Blue is so vital. He's not just coaching for wins; he's coaching for life—mentoring young people to see their value, navigate challenges, and grow into men and women of purpose. In communities where too many kids are overlooked or underestimated, Marc uses sports as both a shield and a springboard. We need more of that. Because when we coach with intention, we don't just change games—we change lives."

Testimonial from NBA Los Angeles Laker Center Jaxson Hayes

"I feel like we need to continue using sports as a tool to reach young people because it teaches them the qualities and what it takes to be successful in life, not just in sports. Sports have taught me how to work hard to succeed and that learning in failure is just as important as winning." Jaxson Hayes

The Legacy You Leave

Ultimately, the true legacy of youth sports lies not in trophies, highlight reels, or scholarship offers. It's found in who these young athletes become, how they grow, how they carry themselves, and how prepared they are to face the world far beyond the scoreboard. *Sports to Life* challenges us to shift the lens from chasing the 2% who make it to the pros to building up the 100% who will become professionals in life as fathers, mothers, leaders, coworkers, and community members!

The lessons learned through sports, such as resilience, time management, emotional regulation, teamwork, and leadership, are among the most transferable skills any young person can acquire. However, for those lessons to stick, coaches, mentors, and educators must intentionally connect them to real-life experiences. We must not assume the game alone will do the teaching. We are the translators between the playbook and real life.

Throughout this book, we've explored the developmental journey of young athletes, including the critical stages of brain growth from ages 10 to 18. Understanding this journey is crucial for any adult working with young people. A 12-year-old who reacts emotionally may not be disrespectful, but they may be overwhelmed by their emotional sensitivity; their brain is still developing the ability to process emotions. A 17-year-old who steps into leadership doesn't just need praise, but they need responsibility. By meeting young people where they are developmentally, we build a bridge between potential and purpose.

But we also acknowledge the double-edged nature of sports. When used intentionally, sports can heal, teach, and uplift. When misused, through toxic coaching, pressure to win, or neglecting emotional well-being, they can damage, exclude, and create long-term wounds. The power of sports is real, and that power can go either way depending on who's holding the whistle.

That's why we introduced the iPlayiLead Academy framework: to provide coaches with a roadmap for utilizing sport as a vehicle for life skills and character development. Through structure, reflection, mentorship, and community partnerships, this model redefines what success looks like in youth sports. It's no longer just about wins and losses, but it's about how many young lives are strengthened and shaped through our programs.

The role of a coach is not just to prepare athletes for the next game, but to prepare them for life. The coaches who understand trauma-informed practices, who know how to build emotional safety, who check in before they call out, and who see their players as whole people, those are the coaches who leave a lasting legacy.

The same goes for program culture. When a team's identity is built on respect, accountability, and compassion, it becomes more than just a team; it becomes a place where young people can safely fail, learn, grow, and belong. And that's the environment where transformation happens.

So, to every coach, mentor, and educator reading this: You may never know the full impact you've had. You may never hear the words "thank you" in the moment. But know this, your influence stretches far beyond the field or court. The habits you teach, the patience you model, the expectations you hold, and the love you show become the foundation of someone's future.

The power of sports is not just in the plays we call. It's in the people we shape, the purpose we plant, and the legacy we leave. Let that be your scoreboard and let that be your win.

MAYE'S 5 KEY CHAPTER TAKEAWAYS: CONCLUSION

1. The true legacy of youth sports is life preparation, not trophies—the real win is in shaping future fathers, mothers, leaders, and community members, not just chasing the small percentage who go pro.

2. Sports skills must be intentionally connected to life—resilience, teamwork, leadership, and emotional regulation only stick when coaches and mentors translate them beyond the game.

3. Youth development is stage-specific—understanding brain growth from ages 10 to 18 helps adults meet young athletes where they are, bridging potential into purpose.

4. Sports hold a double-edged power—when used with care, they can heal and uplift; when misused, they can cause harm and long-term damage to young people.

5. Coaches and culture shape lasting impact—trauma-informed, compassionate coaching and team environments built on respect and accountability create safe spaces for transformation and life-long growth.

Acknowledgments

First and foremost, I give all glory and honor to God for blessing me with this opportunity to share my vision and use my voice to help others. Without His grace and guidance, none of this would be possible.

To my immediate family—thank you for always believing in me, even in the moments when I struggled to believe in myself. Your love and encouragement have carried me further than words can express.

A special thank you to my grandparents, Herman and Delois Maye, who raised me with unconditional love, wisdom, and guidance. You gave me the foundation I needed to stand on, and I will forever honor the sacrifices you made for me.

To my loving sister Michelle, my aunts Alisa, Wendi, and Geia, my uncles Ken, Michael, and Tone Tone, my first cousins Shaqua, Jonathan, Jade, Chance, Calloni, Bailey, Britney, and Carlin — thank you for being my support system and reminding me of the power of family.

To my entire Church of Christ family, thank you for always keeping me grounded in faith and rooted in purpose. A special acknowledgement to the Imperial congregation for being a part of my upbringing and helping me find my purpose in life.

To my Project Blue Team & Board— I'm grateful for your trust in me as a leader and your commitment to walking this journey with me. The work we do is meaningful because we do it together. A heartfelt thank you to Ariel, Yaretzi, Shane, Nellie, Coughlin, Wilhem, Alexis, Patty, and especially Steve and Janet, for being the visionaries behind Project Blue and for allowing me to uplift our community in ways that truly matter.

To my Community Safety Partnership family, thank you for walking the walk alongside me. Together, we are building something greater than ourselves, for the benefit of all.

To my iPlay iLead Academy family — the coaches, kids, parents, and partners — you are the highlight of my weeks. Thank you to Trayonna, Justin, Yaretzi, Orlando, Rashad, Clay, John, Otha, Ean, Destiny, Bobby, Brian, Bryman, Devan, Karin, Amber, Cynthia, Jade, Shakinah, and to every young person who continues to show up with energy and passion. You are the reason this work is worth it.

A very special thanks to Kurt Rambis, Linda Rambis, Kiesha Nix, and the Los Angeles Lakers family for being unwavering supporters of our academy and organization. Your generosity, resources, and commitment to opening doors of opportunity for our community and families have made an immeasurable difference.

To my brother Jaxson Hayes—thank you for being a role model and investing your time in the lives of our kids. I always remind people: children may not remember how much money you spend, but they will never forget how much time you give. You've given so much of yourself, and it has left a lasting impact on their lives.

To Ms. Tina Johnson, thank you for opening the doors of St. Albert the Great and allowing us to provide weekly programming for the community. Your belief in our mission has created an environment where many young people can thrive.

To my St. Lawrence family, thank you for giving me my start, for letting me be me, and for always keeping a door open for me to remain a part of the village that serves our community.

To the Watts Rams and Lincoln Rams programs — what an honor it is to serve two incredible communities that are so passionate, dedicated, and committed to giving back to their community. Thank you for allowing me to help move the impact needle forward for the good.

To my Los Angeles Rams family — especially Molly Higgins, Jonathan Franklin, Andrew Whitworth, and Noel Grigsby — thank you for a partnership that has truly changed lives. Your dedication has provided access and opportunities to youth who might never have had the chance if it weren't for you.

To my CSUDH family, thank you for always being a supportive institution of this work and for creating pathways that encourage every student to dream big and aim high. It is an honor to stand alongside you in endeavors that uplift the community.

To the entire community of Compton and Watts — the two cities I proudly call home — know that I will forever be committed to uplifting you, providing resources and opportunities, and ensuring that respect is always given as it is rightfully deserved. I love every person that makes up these communities, and I promise to always represent with integrity, love, passion, and purpose.

And finally, to all my family and friends — thank you for supporting me on this journey. It is because of you that I keep going.

With gratitude and love,
Marc Maye

About the Author

Marc Maye, a native of Compton, CA, is a passionate advocate for youth development through sports. Having witnessed firsthand the challenges faced by many of his peers due to gang involvement, Marc credits his strong support system and participation in youth and sports programs for his own impactful journey. He earned his Bachelor's in Kinesiology from CSUDH and a Master's in Education from Mount St. Mary's College.

As CEO of Project Blue, Marc is dedicated to strengthening community-law enforcement relationships and closing equity gaps through youth programming. He is also the visionary Founder of 4wrdProgress Youth Foundation, a non-profit committed to teaching and developing essential life skills in young people through sports. Marc's deep commitment stems from a belief in sports as a powerful tool for holistic growth, a philosophy he champions in "The Power of Sports" to empower coaches, mentors, and educators to shape future leaders on and off the field.

Afterword

Wrapping up my senior season as UCLA's all-time leading rusher and being drafted by the Green Bay Packers, I had the perfect roadmap: play for 10 years, then retire, riding the horse into the sunset. What I did not expect was that my NFL career would be cut short due to an injury after 12 games during my rookie season. Life dealt its cards, giving me a hand that I never wanted and expected. Imagine having a dream that you worked fifteen years to achieve, and within 30 seconds, it's taken from you, and there is nothing you could ever do to get it back.

Once my NFL career ended, I was faced with two decisions: to remain in a state of self-pity or to embrace and endure the path set before me. It was challenging to decide what to choose. For the first month, the pain, confusion, fear, and doubt overpowered any inkling to believe that I could find joy again.

No longer having the opportunity to play football was new, but interesting enough, the feelings were familiar. In sports, you're positioned in different situations and challenges that prompt a reaction and decision. Each of these moments, over time, forms the level of character, mindset, discipline, and leadership style that someone has. As I began to rebuild my life after football, I immediately realized the incredible role sports had played in my life.

Sports were not only a driver of success on the field, but also prepared me for wins off the field. The opportunities to lead teams, consistently redefine my own limits, embrace criticism, take accountability for my role in team loses and motivate teammates from diverse backgrounds, set a foundation of character and created the transferrable life skills that I needed to overcome the pain of my unexpected injury but has now carried over to help me thrive in the most important roles I serve in: being a father, husband, leader, friend, and minister. The game has now given me an edge to determine wins and losses in life, and for that, I will forever be grateful.

During a site visit to one of our youth football teams, the Watts Rams, while working for the Los Angeles Rams, I had the opportunity to meet Marc Maye, a beloved leader in the Los Angeles community and a beacon of hope. It became clear to me when I met Marc that his passion and skills are rooted in helping others unlock and maximize their potential. Consistently over the years, I have seen him address players, executives, parents, and coaches in different environments, but the same results happen. Everyone continues to be inspired, well-educated on the specific topics he speaks about, and yearns for more of Marc's wisdom.

This is the sentiment in Marc Maye's inspiring new book, "From Sports to Life! Using Sports to Build Character, not Characters. Through this book, you will understand how sports provide a unique playbook full of keys to succeed in life, shape the mindset of adolescents, teach conflict resolution, how to build culture, develop a strategy, and measure success. Author Marc Maye has helped hundreds of youth, coaches, players, and professionals achieve their goals. From Sports to Life! Using Sports to Build Character, not Characters, is a guide to daily decisions, and a road map to long-term success.

This book is valuable to people of all ages, helping you not only to win within your respective sport and corporation, but also to win in life.

Jonathan Franklin,
Los Angeles Rams Director of Social Justice

"Sports is the greatest metaphor we have for life."

~Kobe Bryant

NOTES

NOTES

NOTES

NOTES

NOTES

NOTES